A Collection of Hieroglyphs: A Contribution to the History of Egyptian Writing

Francis Llewellyn Griffith, Egypt Exploration Fund

ARCHAEOLOGICAL SURVEY OF EGYPT

EDITED BY F. LL. GRIFFITH, M.A., F.S.A.

SIXTH MEMOIR

A COLLECTION OF

HIEROGLYPHS

A CONTRIBUTION TO THE HISTORY OF EGYPTIAN WRITING

BY

F. LL. GRIFFITH

WITH NINE COLOURED PLATES

From facsimiles by

ROSALIND F. E. PAGET, ANNIE PIRIE
AND HOWARD CARTER

SPECIAL PUBLICATION OF THE EGYPT EXPLORATION FUND

LONDON
SOLD AT
THE OFFICES OF THE EGYPT EXPLORATION FUND, 37, GREAT RUSSELL STREET, W.C.
AND AT 59, TEMPLE STREET, BOSTON, MASS., U.S.A.
AND BY KEGAN PAUL, TRENCH, TRÜBNER & CO., PATERNOSTER HOUSE, CHARING CROSS ROAD, W.C.
B. QUARITCH, 15, PICCADILLY, W.; ASHER & CO., 13, BEDFORD STREET, COVENT GARDEN, W.C.

1898

LONDON
PRINTED BY GILBERT AND RIVINGTON, LIMITED,
ST. JOHN'S HOUSE, CLERKENWELL, E.C.

EGYPT EXPLORATION FUND.

CONTENTS.

PREFACE.

THE publication of detailed hieroglyphs, &c., in *Beni Hasan* III., seems to have met a want, to judge by the welcome with which it has been received in the scientific press. The criticisms of MASPERO (*Rev. Crit.*, xliii., pp. 201 *et seqq.*) and BORCHARDT (*Ä. Z.*, 1897, pp. 103 *et seqq.*) have at once displayed how little is positively known with regard to the origins of individual signs, and furnished new material and ideas for the study of them. PIEHL (*Sphinx*, ii., pp. 33 *et seqq.*) has also contributed some suggestions, and M. LORET, in a private letter, has communicated a number of interesting observations on those representing natural objects. At the last moment also appears a long and friendly notice by M. FOUCART in the *Rev. Arch.* (Sér. iii., 1898, vol. xxii., pp. 20 *et seqq.*).

The present work is in continuation of the task begun in *Beni Hasan* III.: that of ascertaining and illustrating the history and origins of the hieroglyphic characters. Much special study has meanwhile been devoted to the subject, and it is hoped that the present Memoir, besides being more elaborate, will show a marked advance in the explanation of the signs upon the somewhat hasty descriptions in the preceding volume.

The greater number of the coloured facsimiles given herewith are from hieroglyphs of the XIIth Dynasty, copied by Mr. H. Carter (a few by Mr. Blackden), in the tomb of Tehutihetep at El Bersheh. This tomb has been already published—in outline only—in *El Bersheh* I. There is also a considerable collection of XVIIIth Dynasty signs from the temple of Deir el Bahri, beautifully copied by Miss R. F. E. Paget. The relief-sculpture and colouring of the inscriptions at Deir el Bahri are well known to be exceedingly fine. The signs selected are from parts of the temple already published by M. Naville, and the originals are in very good preservation. Lastly, Miss A. Pirie has most kindly presented to the Archaeological Survey, for use in the present volume, her facsimile drawings of a number of hieroglyphs from the tomb of Paheri at El Kab. The tomb of Paheri was published in the XIth Memoir of the Egypt Exploration Fund by Mr. J. J. Tylor and myself, as well as separately by Mr. Tylor in an *édition de luxe.* It is of the same age as the temple of Deir el Bahri.

In order to extend the enquiry over a wider field, and so obtain more solid results, the text has not been confined to the new collection of hieroglyphs, but includes most of those already published in *Beni Hasan* III. and in the coloured plates of *Beni Hasan* I.

It will be observed that a special fount of alphabetic hieroglyphs has been made for this volume. This has been done in order to obviate some of the standing difficulties in transliteration, a matter discussed below in the Preliminary Note.

Neat and clear though they be, the founts of general hieroglyphic type now in use are very unsatisfactory. They were modelled on late forms, and often without understanding of the objects and actions which the signs were meant to represent. A few of the most misleading have here been corrected, but materials are not yet available for a thorough revision.

In parting from the pleasant task which has long occupied him, the author would crave indulgence for the many imperfections of his work. After much close application to it, time spent in definite research has often appeared almost wasted when its results were compared with these afterwards obtained casually in pursuing other branches of Egyptology. Scarcely an hour now spent in looking over inscriptions fails to reveal new and often decisive evidence touching upon one or another of the innumerable points of discussion raised in the following pages.

It is useless at present to hope to achieve anything like finality in the study. The whole field needs investigation, and many thousands of good facsimiles are required to put the subject of the origins of the hieroglyphs on a firm basis.

LIST OF ABBREVIATIONS.[1]

TERMINOLOGY.

Ab.	Abbreviation (p. 7).
Alph.	Alphabetic phonogram (p. 3).
Det.	Determinative (p. 5).
Dyn.	Dynasty.
Id.	Ideogram (representing idea, not sound; cf. [pp. 3, 5).
Id. trans.	Ideographic transference (p. 3).
M.K.	Middle Kingdom.
N.K.	New Kingdom.
O.K.	Old Kingdom.
Phon.	Phonogram (p. 3).
Phon. trans.	Phonetic transference (p. 3).
Rad. ext.	Radical extension (p. 3).

REFERENCES.

Ab., i., ii.	MARIETTE, *Abydos*, 2 vols.
Ä. Z.	*Zeitschrift für Aegyptische Sprache*, Berlin.
Ä. T.	LEPSIUS, *Aelteste Texte*.
B. H., i., ii., iii.	*Beni Hasan*, 3 vols. (E.E.F., A.S.)
Bk. of D.	*Book of Dead*, ed. by Budge.
BON., *Sarc.*	BONOMI, *Sarcophagus of Oimenephthah* (i.e. Sety I.).
BREASTED *de Hymnis.*	BREASTED, *de Hymnis in Solem.*
BR., *D. G.*	BRUGSCH, *Dictionnaire Géographique* (with supplement).
„ *Thes.*	„ *Thesaurus.*
„ *Wtb. and Suppl.*	„ *Wörterbuch* and supplement, 7 vols.
Bul. Pap.	MARIETTE, *Papyrus du Musée de Boulaq*, 3 vols.
CH., *Mon.*	CHAMPOLLION, *Monuments de l'Égypte et de la Nubie.*
Dahchour.	J. DE MORGAN, *Fouilles à Dahchour.*
D. el B., i., ii.	*Deir el Bahari*, 2 vols. (E.E.F.).
Deshasheh.	(E.E.F.)
DÜM., *H. I.*	DÜMICHEN, *Historische Inschriften*, 2 vols.
„ *Peduamenap.*	„ *der Grabpalast des Peduamenap*, 3 vols.
„ *Res.*	„ *Resultate der . . . Expedition*, Theil i.
El B., i., ii.	*El Bersheh*, 2 vols. (E.E.F., A.S.).
ERM., *Gr.*	ERMAN, *Aegyptische Grammatik.*
Hetnub graffiti.	BLACKDEN and FRASER, *Hieratic Graffiti from the Alabaster Quarry of Hetnub.*
Horhotep.	In *Miss. Arch.*, Tome i., pp. 135-180.
Illahun.	PETRIE, *Illahun, Kahun and Gurob.*
Kahun.	„ *Kahun, Gurob and Hawara.*
Kah. Pap.	GRIFFITH, *Kahun Papyri.*
Koptos.	PETRIE, *Koptos.*
LANZ., *Diz. d. Mit.*	LANZONE, *Dizionario di Mitologia Egizia.*
L., *D.*	LEPSIUS, *Denkmäler aus Aegypten und Aethiopien.*
Lebensmüder.	ERMAN, *Gesprach eines Lebensmüden mit seiner Seele* (from the *Abhandlungen* of the Berlin Academy, 1896).
LEVI, *Voc.*	S. LEVI, *Vocabolario Geroglifico-Coptico-Ebraico*, 8 vols.
MAR., *Alb.*	MARIETTE, *Album du Musée de Boulaq.*
„ *Cat.*	„ *Catalogue des monuments d'Abydos.*
„ *D. el B.*	„ *Deir el Bahari.*
„ *Mast.*	„ *Les Mastabas de l'Ancien Empire.*
„ *M. D.*	„ *Monuments Divers.*
MASP., *Ét. Ég.*	MASPERO, *Études Égyptiennes*, 2 vols.
„ *Mom. roy.*	„ *Les momies royales de Deir el Bahari* (in *Miss. Arch.*, i.)
„ *Table d'offrandes.*	„ (in *Rev. de l'Histoire des Religions*, 1897-8.)
„ *Trois années.*	„ *Trois années de fouilles* in *Miss. Arch.*, i.
Math. Pap.	EISENLOHR, *Ein Mathematisches Handbuch.*
Medum.	PETRIE, *Medum.*
Mentuhotep.	STEINDORFF, *Der Grab des Mentuhotep.*
Methen.	Dyn. III.—IV.: tomb in L., *D.*, ii., 2 *et seqq.*
Miss. Arch.	*Mission Archéologique Française au Caire, mémoires.*
MORGAN, *Recherches.*	J. DE MORGAN, *Recherches sur les Origines de l'Égypte*, 2 vols.
Naqada.	PETRIE, *Naqada and Ballas.*
Paheri.	Ed. TYLOR and GRIFFITH, in *Ahnas and Paheri* (E.E.F.).
Pap. Any.	*Papyrus of Any* (Brit. Mus.).
„ *Eb.*	*Papyrus Ebers*, 2 vols.
„ *Har.*	*Facsimile of a Papyrus* (Harris) *of the Reign of Rameses III.* (Brit. Mus.).
PETRIE, *Dec. Art.*	PETRIE, *Egyptian Decorative Art.*
„ *T. e. A.*	„ *Tell el Amarna.*
Piankhy.	Stela of Piankhy, in MAR., *M. D.*, Pl. i. *et seqq.*
PRISSE, *Art.*	PRISSE, *L'Art Égyptien*, 2 vols. and text.
„ *Mons.*	„ *Monuments.*
P. S. B. A.	*Proceedings of the Society of Biblical Archaeology.*
Ptahhetep.	Tomb published in QUIBELL, *Ramesseum.*
Pyr.	Pyramid texts (MASPERO, *Les Pyramides de Saqqareh*).
„ *M.*	„ of Merenra.
„ *N.*	„ of Neferkara Pepy II.
„ *P.*	„ of Pepy I.
„ *W.*	„ of Unas (Wnys).
Rec. de Trav.	*Recueil de Travaux relatifs à la Philologie et à l'Archéologie Égyptiennes et Assyriennes.*
Rev. Arch.	*Revue Archéologique.*
Rev. Rel.	*Revue de l'Histoire des Religions.*
ROS., *M. C.*	ROSELLINI, *Monumenti della Egizia e della Nubia: Monumenti Civili.*
„ *M. d. C.*	„ „ „ *del Culto.*
„ *M. S.*	„ „ „ *Storici.*
SCHACK, *Index.*	SCHACK-SCHACKENBURG, *Index zu den Pyramiden texten.*
SCHIAP., *L. d. F.*	SCHIAPARELLI, *Libro dei Funerali*, 2 vols text, 3 vols. plates.
Sebekaa.	Coffin in *Ä. T.*
SH., *Eg. Ins.*	SHARPE, *Egyptian Inscriptions*, 2 series.
SHELLEY, *Birds.*	SHELLEY, *Birds of Egypt.*
Sign pap.	In *Two Papyri from Tanis* (E.E.F.).
Siût.	GRIFFITH, *The Inscriptions of Siût and Der Rifeh.*
Todt.	*Todtenbuch*, ed. by LEPSIUS, by NAVILLE, and by BUDGE (*Book of the Dead*).
Tomb. Sety I.	LEFÈBURE, *Tombeau de Sety I.*, in *Miss. Arch.*, ii.
Trois années.	MASPERO, *Trois années de fouilles*, in *Miss. Arch.*, i.
Una.	Inscription of Una, in MAR., *Ab.*, ii., 44-45.
Z. D. M. G.	*Zeitschrift der Deutschen Morgenländischen Gesellschaft.*

[1] *v.* ADDENDA.

PRELIMINARY NOTE

ON

THE TRANSLITERATION OF EGYPTIAN.

In previous volumes of the Archaeological Survey we have followed the highly conventional transliteration of hieroglyphs into a system of consonants and vowels such as has become customary in England. But since our present discussion involves especially the true powers of the signs and the origin of their phonetic values (as far as we can ascertain them), that system, unchecked, would here be misleading. The roots of Egyptian words, like those of Semitic, consist of a certain number of consonants, and—as perhaps will become clearer on perusal of this Memoir—the phonetic value of almost every sign in hieroglyphic writing corresponds simply to these bare consonantal roots of one, two, or three consonants (or semi-vowels). Any person acquainted with a Semitic language, say Hebrew or Arabic, will comprehend at once the force of these statements as regards both the palaeography and the language. In Egyptian, as in unpointed Hebrew, and Arabic written without vowels, occasionally a semi-vowel is used in good writing to indicate a vowel, but it never becomes a mere vowel-sign. To transliterate  as *āa* in the following pages, without warning, would be as misleading as to transliterate say اعول by *aȧul* in a discussion of the verbal roots and the values of the letters in Arabic. In the latter case, if the vocalization were unknown, no safer transliteration could be given than ʾʿ*wl*: happily in Arabic we are generally saved from such atrocities by the simplicity of its own alphabet, which makes conversion into any other almost superfluous. It is not so with the highly complex hieroglyphic syllabary: in this, for close scientific work, transliteration is constantly a necessity, and occasionally a distressing group of conventional signs, such as ʿꜣ or ʿʾ, seems almost unavoidable.

There is, however, one way out of the difficulty. The hieroglyphic system included twenty-five alphabetic letters, and in them the values of all the phonetic signs of the system can be expressed. They thus provide a very natural means of transliteration. It is not difficult to learn the values of twenty-five pictorial signs, and if words artificially expressed by this alphabet are kept quite distinct from those in genuine hieroglyphic spelling, there seems no objection to their use where European letters fail to satisfy. As Professor Petrie once suggested in discussing this vexed question of transliteration, the distinction can be secured by the use of a specially small type for the hieroglyphic alphabet, which shall at once sufficiently represent the Egyptian signs, distinguish the transliterations from the true words, range with ordinary English type, and be clear and not unpleasing to the eye. Each of the various systems hitherto advocated employs European letters modified by diacritical points, and arouses the wrath of those who have adopted any one of the other systems. In the present work we endeavour to conciliate all: by the side of the inoffensive hieroglyphic transliteration, which represents in fact the basis of every system, we constantly give European spellings, and so we trust that none of our old supporters will be embarrassed by the additional equipment required for working on this branch of Egyptian study.

THE EGYPTIAN ALPHABET.

For the alphabetic signs and their values see Steindorff, *Das Altaegyptische Alphabet und seine Umschreibung, Z. der Morgenl. Gesells.*, xlvi., 709 (cf. *Baedeker Egypt*, 1898, p. cxxiii.); Erman, *Die Umschreibung des Aegyptischen, A. Z.*, xxxiv., 51 (especially valuable for a clear exposition of the consonantal character of 𓄿, 𓇋, 𓅱, 𓂝), cf. *Grammar*, pp. 6-8.

In many cases in the present volume two transliterations into European characters are given side by side, one being consonantal, the other admitting vowels in conformity with the old system. In the following table the third column shows where either of these systems differs from that of Berlin: in the fourth column are given Arabic and Hebrew equivalents of values that cannot be so well expressed in English letters.

	Berlin.	E.E.F.	Semitic.
𓄿	ʾ, ꜣ	ʾ[1] (*a*)	ا, א
𓇋	*j*, *ỉ*, *i̯*	*y* (*ȧ*)	ي
(𓇌	*j*	*y*	ي)
𓏭	*i*, *ï*	*i*	
𓂝	ʿ	ʿ[2] (*ȧ*)	ع, ע
𓅱	*w*, *u̯*	*w* (*u*)	و
𓃀	*b*		
𓊪	*p*		
𓆑	*f*		
𓅓	*m*		
𓈖	*n*		
𓂋	*r*		
𓉔	*h*		ه, ה
𓎛	*ḥ*[3]		ح
𓐍	*ḫ*	*ḫ* (*k͟h*)[4]	خ
𓄡	*ẖ*	*ẖ* (*c͟h*)	
𓊃	*s*		ס
𓋴	*ś*		שׂ
𓈙	*š*	*š* (*s͟h*)	שׁ
𓈎	*ḳ*	*q*[5]	ק
𓎡	*k*		כ
𓎼	*g*		
𓏏	*t*		ت
𓍿	*ṯ*	*ṯ* (*t͟h*)	ث
𓂧	*d*, *ṭ*	*d*	ط
𓆓	*ḏ*, *ẓ*	*z*	ظ

𓏭 is used at the end of a word for the vowel *i* as a distinctive grammatical ending.

𓇌 is a strengthened form of 𓇋, used after the O.K. when 𓇋 had lost the full force of *y*.

𓄿, 𓇋, (𓇌), 𓅱 are weak consonants or semi-vowels. 𓂋 is also a weak consonant; and 𓋴 (prefixed), 𓅓 (prefixed), 𓇋, 𓇌, 𓅱, 𓏭 and 𓏏 (suffixed) are formative letters at the beginning or end of words. All the above may thus sometimes be neglected in deriving phonetic values from words.

𓄿 often changes to 𓇋, and each at times seems less than consonantal.

The distinction—very important in separating roots—between 𓋴 and 𓊃 was lost after the O.K. In the following pages whenever there is uncertainty in this matter we use the combination 𓋴𓊃.

In early texts 𓄡 varies with 𓈙, and in late writing it was confused with 𓐍. In Coptic 𓄡 becomes k͟h, while 𓐍 often becomes s͟h. Thus the sounds represented by 𓄡 and 𓐍 seem to have crossed each other, travelling in opposite directions. To distinguish them as k͟h and c͟h is a mere convention.

𓍿 generally changed to *t*, so that in N.K. 𓍿 often represents 𓏏; but in some words the distinct sound remained firm. 𓆓 became *d* in many words, and varies with 𓂧 even in old texts. In the following pages the use of the combinations 𓍿𓏏, 𓆓𓂧 indicates when the sounds are subject to these changes. 𓂧 is rather *ṭ* than a true *d*.

---

[1] *Alif*, a breathing as support for a vowel; counts as a consonant in Semitic roots (see p. xii.).
[2] *ʿAin*, a peculiar guttural breathing: a strong consonant (nothing to do with *a*; see p. xii.).
[3] *h* is a soft English *h*, *ḥ* a peculiar guttural *h*.
[4] k͟h as in hard German *ch*; c͟h as in soft German *ch*.
[5] *q* is a guttural *k*; *k* is an English *k*.

N.B.—For the practical purposes of teacher or learner, in order to make the unvocalized roots pronounceable, an *e* may be added to any consonant wherever it facilitates the reading: e.g. 𓎛𓏏𓊪 *ḥ(e)t(e)p*; 𓈖𓉔𓅓𓅱 *n(e)h(e)mw(e)*; 𓇋𓅓 *y(e)m*; 𓅓𓇋 *m(e)y(e)*; 𓈖𓅱 *n(e)w(e)*; 𓅱𓈖·𓏏 *w(e)n·t*; 𓂝𓄿 *ʿ(e)ʾ(e)*; 𓏏𓏭𓅱 *tiw(e)*.

NOTE ON THE SEMITIC CONSONANTS *ALIF* AND *'AIN*.

The following rough statements may give some idea of the use of *Alif* and *'Ain*, and of the semi-vowels *w* and *y* in Semitic and Egyptian.

Though regarded as a consonant, the Semitic *alif* (Hebrew *aleph*), like the Greek soft breathing ' and the French *h*, has little or no sound in pronunciation. It is called a guttural, and is often marked by an interruption of sound. It may be defined to be a breathing as the support for a vowel, and is of great importance both as a radical and as a formative sign.

I. As a radical it may support a syllable in the same way as any other consonant. Thus the root *s'l* makes *sa'ala* (*sa·'a·la*), just as *fth̤* makes *fa·ta·h̤a*. When not itself vocalized—i.e. followed by a vowel—*alif* lengthens the preceding vowel in one way or another.

II. Formative *alif*. To take a striking instance of this: when in inflexion a short vowel of any kind—*a*, *e*, *i*, *o*, or *u*—is prefixed for euphonic reasons to a difficult combination of consonants, its presence is indicated in writing by an *alif* written before the radical consonants. This is called "prosthetic *alif*."

III. *Alif* has by nature a particular affinity to the vowel *a*—as *y* has to *i*, and *w* to *u*, so that *a'* = *â*, *iy* = *î*, *uw* = *û*. When not itself vocalized, it especially lengthens preceding *a* to *â*, and hence is used in writing to indicate long *a* (*â*). (So also *y* and *w* are used in writing to indicate *î* and *û*.)

𓄿 seems to correspond to the Semitic *alif*, especially as a radical. There are probably only two cases, each rare and obscure, of its use as a formative; but occasionally it seems to have been written quite superfluously, even in early texts, its feeble value leading to uncertainty or confusion.

𓇋 is properly *y*, but the sounds of 𓄿 and 𓇋 seem to some extent to have changed places in course of time (cf. the case of 𓊃 and 𓐍). 𓇋 is very often omitted in writing at the beginning of a word, and in this situation may often have been reduced to the value of *alif* at a very early period. It is commonly prefixed to a root, and it may be doubted whether it does not, even in early instances, then represent "prosthetic *alif*" (see Sethe, *De Aleph Prosthetico in Lingua Aegyptiaca*).

It is natural that there should now reign some uncertainty about the use of these weak consonants and the signs that expressed them in Ancient Egyptian: even in Semitic grammars there is considerable complexity about the treatment of the mutual relations of *alif* and *y*.

'Ain (Arab., Heb. *'aiyin*) is a peculiar guttural breathing unknown to European languages. It counts as a strong consonant. In Egyptian *'ain* is represented by 𓂝. In the New Kingdom it was weakened, probably owing to the fact that the sound was unpronounceable to some of the mixed population. It was quite lost during the Graeco-Roman period, but was brought into Egypt afresh by the Arabs, and is still constantly heard in Egypt. 𓎛 *ḥ* is related to this guttural.

A COLLECTION OF

HIEROGLYPHS.

CHAPTER I.

INTRODUCTORY.

I.

PREVIOUS WORK ON EGYPTIAN HIEROGLYPHS: MATERIALS AVAILABLE FOR THEIR STUDY.

UNTIL Professor Petrie published his *Medum* and Professor Erman his *Grammar*, no important work on Egyptian hieroglyphic writing had appeared in recent years. Champollion in his *Grammaire Égyptienne*, issued after the author's death in 1836, gave descriptive names to large numbers of the signs. De Rougé, in his *Catalogue des signes hiéroglyphiques de l'imprimerie nationale*, 1851, attached to each of many hundreds of signs and varieties of signs a short description, often very correct. In 1848, to the first volume of Bunsen's *Egypt's Place in Universal History*, Birch contributed a long list of hieroglyphs, with descriptions and statements of their separate phonetic and ideographic values, and this list was revised and enlarged for the second edition in 1867. In the latter year De Rougé again dealt with the subject, and published a *catalogue raisonnée* of the more usual signs in the first *livraison* of his *Chrestomathie Égyptienne.* Useful to the student as these first lists were in the early stages of decipherment, they are now of little value. For, at the time they were made, the fine early forms were mostly unstudied, and the signs were taken without discrimination from texts of all periods; moreover, the outlines of the signs were inaccurately rendered, their colours unnoted, and their phonetic and ideographic powers very imperfectly determined. Thus, whenever doubt was possible as to the object represented by a sign, little external help was forthcoming for correct identification. To a present-day student of the subject, the scholarly understanding of De Rougé and the ingenuity of Birch are apparent, but the aid which they afford him is small.

In 1872, Brugsch, in his *Grammaire hiéroglyphique*, published a useful list of signs with their phonetic and ideographic values, accompanying them with references to his Dictionary, and distinguishing some of the specially early and late forms. In 1878, Rossi, in his *Grammatica Geroglifica*, from the materials thus furnished by Brugsch and others, constructed for the use of students a *catalogue raisonnée* of the most ordinary signs. The plan on which it is carried out is a good one, but the work has little independent value. We may also note the careful list in Lemm's

Aegyptische Lesestücke, 1883. Several bare lists of printers' founts of hieroglyphic signs have been published, e.g. that of F. Theinhardt, at Berlin, arranged by Lepsius, and that of the rich and elaborate fount in the Imprimerie Nationale at Paris, already mentioned, and re-issued without De Rougé's commentary in a second edition.

The only critical list of hieroglyphs with their powers published recently is that of Erman, printed in his *Grammar*. The system by which he classifies the values—obscured in the English edition by the substitution of the term "ideograph" for *Wortzeichen*, "word-sign"—displays the author's keen insight into the nature of hieroglyphic writing, and the list itself is highly suggestive.

The only native list that has come down to us, that of the Sign Papyrus of Tanis (see IXth Memoir of Egypt Exploration Fund), is unfortunately of the Roman Period, when the original meanings of the signs had been well nigh forgotten. It has its own peculiar interest, but seldom furnishes the smallest hint to the seeker after origins. The famous "Hieroglyphics of Horapollo" occasionally contains a reminiscence of true hieroglyphs, but may well be a composition of the Middle Ages embodying the tiny modicum of half-genuine tradition that had survived till then.

Scattered up and down Egyptological literature there are, as may be imagined, many attempts at explaining individual signs. But any endeavour to treat Egyptian hieroglyphs critically, to ascertain their origins, the history of their use, the original distinction or relationship of signs that resemble each other, reveals how little is really known about them. For the study, good examples showing detail and colouring at different periods are needed, and the evidence furnished by form and colour must be checked by examination of their powers in writing.

Professor Petrie's *Medum* is the mainstay of home students in regard to examples of form for the Old Kingdom, but for all periods occasional detailed and trustworthy drawings and photographs are found among the enormous mass of published texts. To these may now be added the 105 coloured signs in *Beni Hasan* III. and still more numerous examples in the present volume. The writer has also had access to the important collection of facsimiles at University College, London, made for Professor Petrie by Miss Paget. A large proportion of these are copied from our own collections from Beni Hasan and El Bersheh, others are from coffins of late period, and have only palaeographical interest, and others again are from earlier coffins in the British Museum. But the flower of the collection consists in exquisite drawings of sculptured hieroglyphs, sometimes with traces of colour, from the tomb of Ptahhetep at Saqqareh, supplemented by a few from other tombs in the same neighbourhood, and from the pyramid of Pepy I. These were all copied on the spot in 1895-6.

In investigating the powers or uses of the signs, dictionaries give most important aid to the student, and it seems ungrateful not to mention them each by name. The keywords to the meanings, viz., the names of the objects or actions depicted, are often exceedingly rare in the texts, and one requires every aid in the search for them. Brugsch's great Dictionary (1867-1882) frequently settles with close accuracy the meanings of the words considered in it, supplying by quotations the proof of his conclusions. Despite its uncritical method of compilation, Levy's bulky Vocabulary (1887-1894), with its two supplements and long tables of signs, is indispensable in this branch of research, since it gives a multitude of references to rare words and forms of words that occur in notable publications of recent date, such as Maspero's edition of the Pyramid Texts. Special indices, such as Stern's excellent Glossary of the Papyrus Ebers, Piehl's Vocabulary of the Harris Papyrus,

Erman's Glossary of the Westcar Papyrus, and Dr. Budge's Vocabulary of the XVIIIth Dynasty "Book of the Dead," are often helpful. Schack's great Index to the Pyramid Texts is as yet unfortunately little more than begun, but the synoptic index of parallel chapters prefixed to the work is of the greatest value in the search for variant spellings.

II.

POWERS OF THE SIGNS: HISTORY OF THEIR EMPLOYMENT.

We will now consider the connexion between the forms and the powers of the Egyptian hieroglyphs, and their use in writing of the best periods.

Following in the main Professor Erman's classification, we can see that the development of the use of the signs was somewhat thus:

At first, a picture-sign was made to stand either simply for the NAME of the object pictured by it, or for that of some state or action which it naturally indicates. Thus, 𓁹 stands for *yr·t* (*ȧr·t*), "eye"; for *ḥnk*, "offer." Such may be said to be the PROPER uses of the picture as a word-sign. Often there may be several Proper values. Undoubtedly the values commonly originate in the names of the objects which the signs represent, but these names are not always traceable. The ancient name may have become obsolete at an early age, or even if it was current in historic times it may happen that it never appears in the inscriptions.

The IDEOGRAPHIC power is often extended or TRANSFERRED widely, and sometimes in a peculiar and rather unexpected way; e.g. when , a pond, or a vessel containing liquid, is taken as the symbol of womanhood; or a bone harpoon-head is used for polished rods, or reed stems, and for burial, as well as for bone and ivory. Mythology and religion naturally played their part in this extension. The griffon vulture, named *nr*, was the emblem of Mut, the mother-goddess, and so stands for her name *mwt* or *m·t*, "mother." Apparently , the cerastes, was a symbol for father; very likely for a similar reason. The ostrich feather, *šw·t* (*shu·t*), is emblem of Maat, goddess of Truth, and stands for her name also. Sometimes one value of a sign (see , , ,) is probably derived from the name of a locality or geographical division of which it represented the badge or symbol, for reasons of religion, mythology, local produce or manufacture.

From its Proper and other name-values the further use of a word-sign developed in two ways, viz., phonetically and ideographically.

I. PHONETICALLY. The word-sign might be employed to write other words of the same essential sound as those expressing its Proper or Transferred senses. Thus, to begin with, it would be used by RADICAL EXTENSION for other forms of the same root, with the formative signs added in writing when necessary, but afterwards by PHONETIC TRANSFERENCE for any homophonous words, whatever their origin and meaning. At length it might become a purely phonetic sign, to represent part only of a word-root, the rest of which would have to be supplied by other phonetic signs. These PHONOGRAMS, which are very limited in number, may indicate one consonant only, in which case they are termed Alphabetic; or more than one, in which case they are termed Syllabic. There is no further essential difference between alphabetic and syllabic characters.

The origin of many of the alphabetic values is still obscure, but it does not seem likely that the Egyptians ever consciously resorted to the principle of acrophony, i.e. of assigning to a symbol the value of the first only of several sounds in the word which it represents. In the Old Kingdom there are no homophones among the regular alphabetic characters. Of these there are twenty-five, including the vowel-sign 𓏭; but this was not used as such until the Middle Kingdom. The "syllabic" phonograms in regular use at a good period do not much exceed 40.

It is interesting and essential to further research to note the principles on which signs were employed for the expression of sound.

It was convenient as well as natural to employ a given word-sign for all forms of the root to which the word itself belonged. In the (sub-Semitic?) language spoken by the Egyptians the root of each word lay in consonants, and the inflexions no doubt consisted largely in vowel-changes, though these are not traceable in hieroglyphic writing. For instance, the root *ḥtp* might perhaps take, amongst others, such forms as *ḥôtep*, *ḥatp*, *ḥotpe*, *ḥtêp*. Likewise, from the root *rwd* (which we conventionally write *rud*) might be forms *rôwed*, *rawd* (reduced to *raud*, the vowel and semi-vowel coalescing and forming a diphthong), *rowde* (reduced to *rûde*), *rewêd*. And from *wn* (which we conventionally write *un*) there might be *wôn*, *wan*, *owne* (reduced to *ûne*), and *wên*. Possibly, under special circumstances depriving the word of all accent ("construct" state), some form of *wn* might be reduced to a mere *un*; yet radically *w* and *n* would be recognized as still underlying. Thus, 𓊵 "offering," "to be propitiated," stands for 𓎛𓏏𓊪 *ḥ-t-p*; 𓍿 "firm," "knot," stands for 𓂋𓅱𓂧 *r-w-d*; 𓃹 "run like a hare," stands for 𓅱𓈖 *w-n*.

Inflexion and derivation, however, also consisted in the addition of certain consonants, viz., *ś* prefixed (for the causative form), *m* prefixed, an added *t*, *w*, or *y*. Thus, when the word-sign was used for all forms of the word, the vocalization and the flexional and formative consonants had to be abolished from its value and the radical consonants alone retained. When we remember the readiness with which the Arab recognizes the few radical consonants upon which his highly organized verbal conjugations are built, we can better understand the ease with which the Egyptians reduced their word-signs to their radical values. The gradual development of a phonetic system would enable them in course of time to supply the flexional consonants by the addition of separate phonograms. Let us take as an illustration the sign 𓎟. This represents a basket, and the root of the Egyptian name is *nb*, "hold," with the feminine termination *t* = *nb·t*, "the holder." The sign very naturally was required to spell *nb* or *nb·w*, "holder, master" (masculine), *nb·t*, "holder, mistress" (feminine), *nb·w*, "holders, masters" (masc. plural). Hence 𓎟 by itself may stand for a "basket," *nb·t*; it may also stand for "master," and, with the addition of 𓏏 *t*, for *nb·t*, "mistress," or with the addition of 𓅱 *w*, for *nb·w*, "masters." When this stage had been reached, the sign 𓎟 was easily applied to the spelling of a verb *nb*, "swim," and of another verb *nb*, "melt," each with a number of vowel inflexions that we cannot now follow, owing to the incomplete record of sounds in hieroglyphics. We thus see that when a sign is employed for its phonetic value, it is used to represent the skeleton only of the word for which it stands, i.e. the unvocalized and uninflected root (*v.* Addenda).

Even the root was generally reduced to its simplest form, for through inherent weakness of consonants or the coalescence of the last two radicals in any root in which they happened to be identical (cf. Semitic *secundae geminatae*) there might be a shortened form of the root itself. Thus the hoe 𓌸, 𓎛𓈖𓈖 *ḥnn* (*ḥenen*), has the syllabic value *ḥn*; and several of the alphabetic signs appear to owe their value to a single geminated root letter: see description of 𓊃, 𓎡, 𓍘 below, pp. 45, 47, 38. On the other hand, the plant or rush 𓈖𓈖𓏏 *nn·t*, used for 𓈖𓈖 *nn*, has to be doubled in writing, evidently because its value would otherwise be reduced to *n* (see below, p. 29).

The WEAK CONSONANTS are 𓄿, 𓇋, 𓅱 and 𓂋. They seem to have been more or less fugitive according to circumstances. Terminal *r* in many cases where it is found in the earliest texts was lost, or changed to a vowel in course of time. Thus 𓁷𓏤, 𓁷𓂋 *ḥr*, "face," became *ḥ*[*r*], with the *r* changed perhaps to *y*, to which it had a tendency. And if in good writing, after the earliest times were passed, it was required to write a word or syllable *ḥr* with a strong *r*, the spelling had then to be 𓁷𓂋. So also with 𓉐𓏤 *p*[*r*], "house," 𓈘𓏤 *m*[*r*], "channel," &c. But 𓁹 *yr* retains its *r*, because the name of the eye was *yr·t*, and the presence of the feminine ending 𓏏, preceded by a vowel, saved the weak final radical. The effects of final *r* are best studied in phonograms of two consonants, because of the frequency with which they enter into combinations, but doubtless it prevailed also with word-signs of three consonants.

Final 𓄿 (*aleph*), 𓇋 (*yod*), and 𓅱 (when radical) could often likewise be neglected, as might be judged from Semitic analogies, though in what degree still remains to be ascertained. In the Pyramid Texts 𓐍, 𓐍𓄿, is used alternatively for *kh*, and 𓉔 *h* seems to have been originally 𓉔𓄿, and 𓎼 *g*, 𓎼𓄿. Initial 𓇋 is often negligeable, but in such cases it is perhaps not radical. It has long been seen that 𓇋 must often be a euphonic prefix like the prosthetic *alif* in Semitic, and in that position it is always weak and liable to change or disappear.

Changes take place also among the STRONG CONSONANTS; thus, in most roots in course of time 𓎛 changes to 𓂋, here indicated by 𓎛, and 𓊃 to 𓏏, here indicated by 𓊃.

The distinction between 𓋴 and 𓊃 was altogether lost after the Old Kingdom. For vast numbers of words we can verify the ancient form by means of the Pyramid Texts, but in the case of many words not found in the Old Kingdom, we cannot tell which *s* is correct. Such cases are here indicated by 𓊃.

When the two allied consonants 𓂝 and 𓇋 came together in a word, these being difficult so to pronounce, the 𓂝 was, in the Middle Kingdom, often written 𓇋, and, generally, there is some uncertainty about their use. Cf. …; also … The last sign is in many words 𓂝𓇋𓂝, but in "navy" it is 𓇋𓂝.

With other consonants also there are early instances of change or loss, especially perhaps in the case of 𓈖, but at present they have not been reduced to rule, and are altogether obscure.

II. IDEOGRAPHICALLY a sign becomes a DETERMINATIVE, i.e. it is placed after a word spelled in phonograms or in word-signs, in order to indicate the meaning of that word, either in general or specifically. 𓀀 is the determinative of proper names of men, 𓁐 of those of women, &c. 𓃒 is a specific determinative of words meaning ox, bull, &c., but 𓄛, a hide, is a general determinative for all beasts, and may follow the name of any. The use of determinatives is found to decrease the further one goes back into antiquity, and this, as Erman remarks in his Grammar, shows the comparative lateness of their use, and agrees with their natural place in the evolution of the script. From picture-signs derive word-signs, from word-signs phonograms, and then recourse is again had to picture signs, or at least ideograms, for determinatives to phonograms.

The development of the hieroglyphic system of writing did not take place according to rule, and the employment of the signs cannot be completely and neatly tabulated even for a single period of the writing. We may in a general way distinguish Classical from Archaic usage, the spelling in the Old Kingdom being very variable, while in the Middle Kingdom it had become more or less fixed in principle and so continued into the New. Some special developments and usages are as follows:—

1. In classical writing strong flexional consonants are as a rule written separately from the word-sign. Thus , in the Old Kingdom may often stand for *yr·t* (*år·t*), "eye," but later the spelling is . Even in late writing, however, if no ambiguity can result and conciseness is aimed at, the word-sign alone is made to stand for a derived form with a strong consonant. This is the case not only with the of the fem. ending, as , for *n·t*, "city," but also with prefixed ; as when , *ḥnk*, stands for *m·ḥnk* in a certain title (Sethe, *Ä. Z.*, 1893, p. 99), and , *ʿd* (*åd*), stands for *m·ʿd* (*m·åd*), in the name of the sun-boat. So also the scribe's palette, *nʿʿ* (*nåå*), constantly stands for the causative *ś·nʿʿ* (*ś·nåå*), "grind fine," in the prescriptions of the Ebers Medical Papyrus. Again, the knot, properly *ʾyr* (*aår*), stands for *dyʾr* (see below, p. 44). Here *dyʾr* is treated as a derivative of *ʾyr*, and is perhaps so in reality.

It is a remarkable fact that the flexional or formative consonants *m*, *t*, *w*, *y*, even when radical, are apt to drop out of writing, probably by a kind of "false analogy." This may help to explain the occasional omission of at the beginning or in the middle of words, and of at the end, and the constant omission of and in early writing, while always stands firm at the beginning of words.

2. Sometimes a word-sign, say of two radicals, not being a phonogram, was used in spelling another word of three, which happened to have the appearance of a derivative from the biliteral root, a formative consonant being prefixed or suffixed. Thus "fear" is sometimes written , as if *ś·nz*; "strong," , as if *n·ḥt* "of wood"; "statue," , as if derived from *ḥn*; these, and others, may probably be considered as "false derivatives." It is often difficult to say where word-sign ends and phonogram begins.

3. There are two phonograms which are used solely for marking inflexions. The eagle (p. 19), *tiw*, stands for the plural ending of adjectives in *ti*, and as a phonogram is *i*, chiefly as the termination of the dual, and of adjectives derived from substantives. (in good texts is used only for terminations, or at most as a substitute for *final* radical or ; when it replaces the sound of the latter, is generally written as well. In the special spelling for foreign names in the New Kingdom it is used for *y* in any position.)

Certain vowel-endings, being of particular importance, were rendered by special devices. Thus the dual and the adjectival formative *i* was in the Old Kingdom sometimes rendered by , and the same dual ending and the termination of adjectives by (in *Pyr.* and *Una*, l. 30); later, took the place of these. sometimes represents the vowel *u* as masc. sing. termination of nouns. In the New Kingdom the attempt was made to spell foreign names in open syllables of a consonant and a vowel, the latter being represented by , , or (see Erman, *Gram.*, § 70).

4. When an ideogram or a phonetic sign has several values, or when it closely resembles in writing that is not detailed another ideogram or phonetic sign with a different value, a phonetic complement was attached to it in the classical period, as a constant indicator; e.g. *stn* is , *św* , *ḥsf* , *ḥz* .

5. Occasionally a sign ideographic of a *group* of ideas is used to indicate particular words belonging to that group, by the help of one or more phonograms which point out the special meaning. In such cases the ideogram is not merely a determinative, nor yet quite a word-sign. Thus the club (see *B. H.*, iii., fig. 77), ideogram or determinative of foreign peoples,

cannot by itself stand for the name of any foreign people; but , , , (*Una*, l. 16) = , these words meaning respectively "Semite," "Libyan," "negro," and "Libya." It is possible that originally the form of the club may have varied to indicate the particular race, and that the phonetic complements were added when this distinction became too precarious in free writing. The use of (*q.v.*) in its phonetic compounds for verbs of motion is on the same principle.

6. ABBREVIATIONS of various kinds are used in writing accounts, and also in other writing. Sometimes a determinative stands for the whole word, as—in accounts— for , *dmz*, "total"; or the principal sign alone is written, as in the group for , , (*ȧnkh*, *uza*, *senb*), "Life, Prosperity, Health." Incomplete writing of one sort or another is very common (cf. ERMAN, *Defective Schreibungen*, *Ä. Z.*, 1891, p. 33).

7. Sometimes, even in good writing, the word-sign or determinative of a word is transferred as determinative (not word-sign) to a homophonous word to which its meaning is not appropriate; e.g. in "hand," in "flax." It then seems determinative of sound, not of sense. In hieratic of the New Kingdom such uses are very common.

8. Sometimes we have a MONOGRAM or GRAPHIC COMPOUND of two phonetic signs, each to be read separately, as in *ḥt-ḥr*, "Hathor"; of an ideogram or syllabic with its phonetic complement, as in *ḥz*, "white"; or of an ideogram or phonogram with its determinative, as in *ḥz*, "silver." These are written respectively , , .

9. There are also "SPORTIVE" hieroglyphs (ERMAN, *Gram.*, § 71). These are often exceptional signs, and always used in an exceptional way, either because of some magical power attributed to them, or in order to present the reader with a puzzle for his amusement, or for his bewilderment—as in secret writing. Groups written with such hieroglyphs occur in the Kahun Medical Papyrus, the Ebers Medical Papyrus, and the Rhind Mathematical Papyrus. Short inscriptions in the same style are found at Beni Hasan in the tomb of Chety, and at El Bersheh in the tomb of Tehutihetep, and long mythological ones in the tombs of the Kings of the XIXth and XXth Dynasties at Thebes.

10. In the Pyramid Texts signs representing human beings are systematically deprived of their bodies and legs, so that only heads and arms appear. The animals are generally treated in the same way, and and are often cut in two. Apparently this was an attempt to deprive the signs of magic motion. Similarly, in funerary texts of the Middle Kingdom, birds and animals are sometimes deprived of their legs and serpents of their tails. These mutilated signs are of course to be read as though they were complete, and may, for the purposes of this volume, be treated as identical with the complete signs to which they correspond.

Various other tricks of the scribes may be detected. The transferred use of ideograms, and the different employments of certain signs as phonograms, vary with the period and even with the individual scribe. At some periods certain word-signs were employed as phonograms which are not so found at other periods; e.g. , commonly used as phonogram for *ḫ'* (*kha*) in the Pyramid Texts, has elsewhere a very restricted use until the end of the New Kingdom.

It may almost be presumed that the farther we push back into antiquity the greater exactitude shall we find in the use of the signs. To the early scribes each sign had a distinct meaning connected with its origin, but with the development of cursive writing, and indeed the spread of writing into common use, the scribe gradually made himself independent of the delicate differences which distinguished the forms of allied signs. The tendency was to express words either by one distinct sign or by a group so arranged that the meaning would be unmistakable, even when the individual signs might be confounded. This led to a larger use of determinatives and of phonetic complements, and eventually to a handling of signs as conventional symbols even in hieroglyphic writing, and to the forgetting of their origins. Even in good writing of the Middle Kingdom improper use of the signs had crept in, and in the XVIIIth Dynasty this is still more marked. Thus, for example, in the early times the sprout (?) ɩ, having the two values ⌓ ⬭ *tr* and ⬭ ⌐ ▫ *rnp*, was often compounded with an alphabetic catch-sign, ⬭ or ▫, to show the value, and the fem. ⬭ ⌐ ▫ · ⌓ *rnp·t* was generally compounded with ⌓ (see below, p. 26). In the Middle Kingdom these began to be confounded; in the New Kingdom the compound for *tr* was used for *rnp*, and even that for *rnp* was used for *tr*, although the latter had no *p*. The sound and meaning of each word being obvious from the more systematic spelling out by a group of several signs, there was little practical importance in the distinction between ɩ and ɩ▫.

As might be expected, the colouring and details of the signs of which the origin was not very obvious, were given with less and less intelligence. In the following pages few references occur to the uses and forms of signs after the XXth Dynasty. By that time corruption had set in strongly from various causes, and there is seldom much trustworthy light to be obtained from examples of this date on the original significance of the signs. To trace the origin and history of each sign minutely through its different uses and forms, from the earliest times to the latest, would be a stupendous work, analagous to the construction of an elaborate dictionary "on historical principles." But even from brief excursions into this comparatively untrodden field of research, much new information may be gained and many current errors corrected.

CHAPTER II.

HIEROGLYPHS COLLECTED BY THE ARCHAEOLOGICAL SURVEY.

I.
SOURCES OF THE FACSIMILES.

PLATES I.-IV.—HIEROGLYPHS OF THE XVIIITH DYNASTY, FROM DEIR EL BAHRI. COPIED BY MISS R. F. E. PAGET.

These hieroglyphs are of the age of Hatshepsut, fourth monarch of the XVIIIth Dynasty (about 1520 B.C.), and were copied in her great temple in the winter of 1895-6. The originals were first sculptured in relief and then coloured. All those here published are from portions of the temple already described and published by M. Naville in his memoir on Deir el Bahari, Parts I. and II. The greater number are from the chapel of Thothmes I., but some are from scenes not included in the plates of the memoir. In this chapel, according to M. Naville (*D. el B.*, i., p. 4), the transparent varnish with which the paint was overlaid has turned to an opaque yellow. The effects of this are seen on many of the hieroglyphs here published, in which the white ground is smudged with yellow or the original colours obscured and altered, e.g. Pl. iv., figs. 23, 27-29, 40, &c., &c. Some of our examples are from the North-West Hall of Offerings, and others from the Birth Terrace, from an inscription parts of which have escaped mutilation. The positions of the originals are as follows:—

Altar Court, fragmentary inscription, unpublished (cf. *D. el B.*, i., Pl. v., &c.), fig. 30.

Chapel of Thothmes I.:
- Position uncertain, fig. 35.
- End wall (*D. el B.*, i., Pl. ix.), figs. 6-9, 15-21, 26, 31, 32, 49.
- East wall (*D. el B.*, i., Pl. x.), figs. 27-29, 50. (*D. el B.*, i., Pl. xi.), figs. 1, 2, 13-14, 23, 25.
- West wall, unpublished, figs. 10-12, 37-39, 46.
- Niche, North wall (inscription beyond *D. el B.*, i., Pl. xv.; cf. Pl. xvi.), figs. 5, 34, 43, 45.
- Niche, South wall (*D. el B.*, i., Pl. xvi.), figs. 3, 22, 40, 41.

North-West Hall of Offerings:
- West or East wall (*D. el B.*, i., Pl. xix. or xxii.), fig. 36.
- West wall (*D. el B.*, i., Pl. xxi.), fig. 24.

Middle Colonnade, northern half (*D. el B.*, ii., Pl. xlviii., right-hand end), figs. 4, 33, 42, 44, 47, 48.

PLATES V.-VI.—HIEROGLYPHS OF THE XVIIITH DYNASTY, FROM THE TOMB OF PAHERI AT EL KAB. COPIED BY MISS A. PIRIE.

From the table of his genealogy it is evident that Paheri died in or about the reign of Hatshepsut and Thothmes III. (*Paheri*, p. 9). As the decoration of the tomb was probably not finished much before his death, it is therefore of almost precisely the same date as the temple of Deir el Bahri. The small inscriptions in the chamber are incised and coloured black, but the large ones are well formed in relief and coloured. There are no indications that the tomb-chamber was ever closed or hidden, and the destruction of the façade has exposed it to the full effects of atmosphere, wind, and wind-borne sand. Although as a whole the sculptures are in excellent preservation, the colour and relief have suffered considerably in detail. In the winter of 1896 Miss Pirie, who was staying at El Kab, copied some of the signs and kindly gave the copies to the Archaeological Survey. The exact situation and context of each of these signs was carefully noted, and this precaution adds considerably to the value of the examples. No great accuracy was observed by the draughtsman or sculptor in the use of the signs. The  of 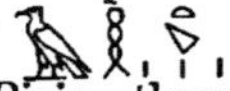 (Pl. iii., top left), copied by Miss Pirie, though not here published, is the brown "eagle," rather than the Egyptian vulture, and on Pl. x., east side, we have  instead of  as determinative of 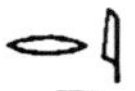 in the name .

The positions of the originals are as follows in the plates of *Paheri*, all being from the interior of the chamber:—

Front wall, Pl. ii., fig. 51.
West wall:
- Pl. iii., cornice line, figs. 57, 59, 60, 62, 70, 71, 77, 83.
  - upper left, figs. 63, 66, 69.
- Pl. iv., cornice line, figs. 61, 64, 72, 75, 78.
  - upper middle, figs. 53, 67, 76.
  - lower right, fig. 52.

East wall:
- Pl. vi., offerings, figs. 79, 81.
  - upper left, fig. 80.
- Pl. vii., cornice line, fig. 56.
  - upper left, figs. 68, 73, 74.
- Pl. viii., cornice line, figs. 55, 65, 82.
  - upper left, fig. 58.
  - middle, fig. 54.

Plates VII.-IX.—Hieroglyphs of the XIIth Dynasty, from the Tomb of Tehutihetep at El Bersheh. Copied by Mr. Howard Carter and Mr. M. W. Blackden.

The completion of the tomb of Tehutihetep must be dated in the reign of Usertesen III., the fifth king of the XIIth Dynasty (*El B.*, i., Pl. v., and p. 3). Our collection of signs from it was begun by Mr. Blackden, who in December, 1892, copied six, which I believe he found on fallen fragments of the painting. The remainder, 104 in number, were copied chiefly from the walls of the tomb by Mr. Carter in May and June, 1893. All are from the inner chamber, but their precise positions are generally difficult to identify.

Good examples of most of the facsimiled signs may be found in *El B.*, i., Pls. xv., xviii., xx. (right side), xxii.; the originals of several of the hieroglyphs were probably on small fragments, which have not been included in the plates of that memoir. In the following cases, however, the exact positions of the originals may be noted:—

El Bersheh I.:
- Pl. xii., right, fig. 126.
- Pl. xv., row 1, fig. 161.
  - row 2 (or 3 ?), fig. 147.
  - row 3, fig. 148.
  - row 4, fig. 149.
  - row 5, left, figs. 158, 191.
- Pl. xviii., row 1, figs. 154-156.
  - row 3, figs. 119, 179, 180.
- Pl. xx., right, figs. 90, 97, 98, 136, (top) 150.
- Pl. xxv., figs. 122, 186.
- Pl. xxxiv., top, fig. 118.

Not in the publication(?), figs. 86, 165, 167, 190.

Facsimiles previously Published.

Beni Hasan, i., Pls. xxvii., xxviii. These two coloured plates are taken from the tomb of Chnemhetep (temp. Usertesen II.). They contain several interesting hieroglyphs.

Beni Hasan, iii., Pls. i.-vi. (See *B. H.*, iii., p. 3). The dates of the tombs in which the hieroglyphs were copied are as follows (for the proofs, see *B. H.*, i., pp. 7 *et seqq.*):—

Tomb 17, of Chety; end of XIth Dynasty.

Tomb 14, of Chnemhetep; Amenemhat I. (first king of XIIth Dynasty).

Tomb 2, of Amenemhat; Usertesen I. (second king of XIIth Dynasty).

Tomb 3, of Chnemhetep; Usertesen II. (fourth king of XIIth Dynasty): it is thus very nearly contemporary with the tomb of Tehutihetep at El Bersheh.

II.

DISCUSSION OF THE SIGNS IN NATURAL GROUPS.

A. Humanity.

Fig. 184. Man seated on the ground in the usual attitude, i.e. kneeling on one knee, both arms bent, with hands closed as if in effort to rise (?).

In O.K. occasionally perhaps word-sign for *s*, "man," "person," and repeated for *rmt*, in the sense of "men" (*Una*, l. 21). After O.K., id. of first pers. sing. masc., standing for its suffix, *y* (*á*). It is det. of male persons in general, and in particular is used regularly after proper names, except in the earliest period.

Fig. 152; *B. H.*, iii., fig. 79. Woman seated on the ground, closely wrapped, with long wig hanging over back [and shoulders].

Probably occurs as word-sign for *ḥm·t*, "woman." Corresponds precisely to in all its uses as suffix and det.

Group of man and woman; with plural sign after O.K. (figs. 184 and 152 were taken from this group in *El B.*, i., Pl. xv.).

Word-sign for *rm·t*, "people" (e.g. *Kah. Pap.*, p. 35). Det. of human beings in general, of their classes, tribal names, &c.

Fig. 162. A baby, as carried by its nurse, sucking its finger [and with a lock of artificial hair hanging from one side of its head].

Word-sign for *ẖrd* (*c̲hred*), "child": in the name of Heracleopolis Magna, *Ḥwn(?)·n·śtn* (*Ḥunenśeten*), it is regularly written, apparently for "youth," *ḥwn* (Brugsch, *Ä. Z.*, 1886, p. 76, from a variant *ḥn* in *Todt.*, cap. 125, l. 9). In *B. H.*, i., Pl. xxxii., in a group corresponding to *B. H.*, i., Pl. xxvi., l. 189, it stands by exception for *nẖn* (*nek̲hen*), "infancy," "innocence," "simplicity." In late times it was used for *ms*, "child," *s*ᵓ (*sa*), "son."

Figs. 25, 182. Front view of human face, showing ears and artificial beard.

Properly *ḥr*, "face," lit. "the upper (thing)"; written , which is also the preposition *ḥr*, "upon."

The final *r* was soon weakened or lost; and in employing it as a word-sign, almost if not quite as a phon., it was usual, except at the earliest period, to add in writing if the *r* remained strong. Thus , not , is the regular spelling for *ḥr*. The use of for *ḥ*[*r*] is probably restricted to the two words already mentioned.

Fig. 59. Upper part of face, showing nose and eye in profile.

Name *ḫnt* (*k̲hent*), with radical *t*, lit. "the foremost (part of the face)"; cf. especially *Pyr. M.*, l. 306. In late texts it is word-sign for *ḫnt*. Gradually it was substituted for other signs ideographic of the nose, and so stood for its name *fnz*, "nose," and for *šn*, "smell," *ššn*, "breathe." Thus it became det. of all actions of the nose — smelling, breathing, kissing—sometimes also of pleasure, festivity, disgust, and of gentle behaviour (?) ( ).

Figs. 19, 188. The human eye.

Name, *yr·t* (*ȧr·t*), see SPIEGELBERG, *Rec. de Tr.*, xvii., 93: written , (*Pyr.*), and . Common phon. for *yr* (*ȧr*). Det. of words of seeing, not uncommonly.

[*B. H.*, iii., fig. 60.] Side-view of mouth.

In *El B.*, i., Pl. xxvii., the title written with this sign in *B. H.*, i., Pl. xxx., is rendered with (*q.v.*), which in that instance may very well represent the outline of the lips. In any case, the word probably reads *ḫn(r)·t* or *ḫn·t* (*khen·t*).

Fig. 157; *B. H.*, iii., fig. 57. Lips of human mouth, slightly open (interior white).

Name, *r*, "mouth," Copt. ⲣⲱ. Word-sign for prep. *r*, "to," and alph. for *r*.

Fig. 100; *B. H.*, iii., fig. 59. Human arm to above the elbow, showing hand outstretched.

Name, ʿ (*ȧ*), "hand," presumably including a portion above the wrist. There is, however, little difference of meaning between and as word-signs, and in parallel texts they are sometimes interchanged (cf.). is alph. for ʿ (*ȧ*), Arab. ع, Heb. ע. In *Pyr.* it appears to stand often for *rmn*, "forearm," or "upper arm" (?)—later, —and is then usually distinguished by alphabetic complements or . Sometimes it takes the place of for the "cubit," *mḥ*, and of "give."

As det. it is also substituted for , and for (*q.v.*).

Fig. 172; *B. H.*, iii., fig. 53. Human hand, open.

Name, *d·t*, "hand," lit. probably "the giving," or "placing (thing)"; just as the palm is called "the receiving (thing)" (*v.*), the shank "the running (thing)" *wʿr·t* (*uȧr·t*), and the thigh "the firm (thing)" *mn·t*. The name of the numeral 5 is perhaps connected with it, but the pronunciation of this is not certain; perhaps it may be *dwꜣ* (*dua*); cf. ★ below. In *Pyr.*, as a verb, varies with *wd* (*ud*); cf. MASP., *Ét. Ég.*, ii., 123.

From the above name of is derived its value as alph. for *d* (or rather for *ṭ*, Ar. ط).

Fig. 131. The human foot and leg from below the knee. In inscriptions of Dyn. I. the form is (DE MORGAN, *Recherches*, ii., fig. 786), but the length of the shank was quickly increased, and this part of the sign soon became disproportionately long and slender.

Since , is alph. for *b*, we may probably assume this to be derived from an ancient word for "foot," or something similar; the common word for foot is *rd*, in which the sign shows the leg above the knee, so that and might correspond in the same way as and for "hand." There is in fact a common word *bw* (*bu*), written in N.K. but almost invariably in early texts (for *Pyr.* see SCHACK, *Index*) that seems to be the origin of the alphabetic value. It means "place," "situation," "condition," especially in expressions like *bw nfr*, "good state," "felicity," &c.; perhaps we may compare the English "footing" for *status*. The compound *bw nb* means "everybody," which may be literally "every condition or class," or perhaps better "every foot," like

, another compound expression for "everybody," lit. "every face."

It may be noted that in *Pyr.* is det. of a word , (*T.*, 312, &c.), which perhaps means "footstep," "tread," or "foot," and of "sandal."

B. Anthropomorphic Deities; Human Ranks and Classes.

Fig. 149. Human figure seated on the ground, closely wrapped, with ibis-head or mask and heavy wig.

Word-sign for Thoth. In the tomb of Tehutihetep, who was priest of this great god at the centre of his worship in Upper Egypt, the sign is used as det. of *ntr*, "god," as well as of the name of Thoth.

The representation of Thoth as an ibis-headed man occurs as early as the IVth Dyn., L., *D.*, ii., 2, *c*. This raises the question whether the early Egyptians did not conceive of the god as existing in this form; but the type may very well have arisen as a graphic compound of the figure of the (anthropomorphic) god with that of his sacred bird to distinguish him from other gods. So also with Anubis, Ra, &c. The det. of a god's name is commonly .

Fig. 21. A bearded figure, seated, i.e. kneeling on one knee, arms extended and hands raised, perhaps to symbolize counting by tens; on his head the symbol of a year or season. There is also the form (*Siut*, tomb i., l. 227, &c.).

This god or symbolical figure is represented in the vignettes of the *Todt.*, cap. xvii., as a god of moisture, and in *Pap. Any*, Pl. viii., his name is given *Ḥeḥ*. His function is well shown in the birth scene at Luxor (L., *D.*, iii., 74, *c*), where two such figures uphold the symbol of life. At Deir el Bahri (*D. el B.*, ii., Pl. li.), the two figures are so small that they might be taken for mere symbols, but at Luxor they are of full figure size. Thus it may seem that the sign represents a god of long life, of a multitude of years. On the other hand, he seems to be also the god of teeming productiveness.

Ḥḥ, , means a "vast number," and is an expression for higher numbers than 100,000 (Mar., *D. el B.*, Pl. viii.; L., *D.*, iii., 77, *c*); but its sense, like that of Ω, was rather vague, and it is never used in real accounts.

Fig. 148. The figure of a king with uraeus on forehead, false beard, wig, and pigtail, seated on the ground and closely wrapped, his hand alone appearing and holding the (*q.v.*). Usually he holds the crook likewise.

In *El B.*, i., Pl. xv., row 3, this figure is det. of the word *yty* (*àty*), "king." It is the usual det. of royalty, and is the royal sign of the pronominal suff. of first pers. sing.

Fig. 161. A person of high rank walking with tall staff in one hand and mace (?) in the other. The sign usually has the addition of ram's horns and two plumes on the head, (*Pap. Any*, Pl. i., l. 8).

Usual det. of the word *yty* (*àty*), "king."

Fig. 147. A beardless figure, completely enveloped, except head and arms; seated on a chair with animal legs and ornament like a papyrus-head behind; over the low back a cloth or skin.

In *El B.*, i., Pl. xv., this sign is det. of "master," and "father"; possibly it indicates that they were deceased, or it may signify that those persons were such as were to be treated with respect.

[*B. H.*, iii., fig. 74.] Watchman. The object on the staff here resembles , but the form varies greatly (cf. *Medum*, Pls. xxii., xxviii., and the figure in the boat, Pl. xxiv.). Cf. also , p. 62.

Word-sign for *s'w* (*sa'u*), "watchman," with phon. trans.; and for *yri* (*ȧri*), "concerned with." The fem., *yr't*, is often written with a female form.

Fig. 159. Soldier holding bow and quiver full of arrows; lightly clothed and kneeling on one knee in an attitude of alertness; generally wearing a feather, cf. *Medum*, ix., &c.

Word-sign for "host," "infantry," "soldiers," and for an "expedition" with an army, either for peaceful objects—quarrying and conveying stone—or for war; apparently it never stands for a single soldier, except as det. of the name *ʿḥ'w'ti* (*ȧḥauti*), lit. "fighter."

BRUGSCH, *Ä. Z.*, 1880, p. 8, and PIEHL, *l.c.* p. 135, have shown that the title in the XXXth Dyn. varies with , *mr šs* (*mer shes*), and that is actually at that time written for , *šs* (*shes*), "rope" or "fine linen." Apparently, therefore, *šs* is the reading of this sign. It is at present generally read *mšʿ* (*meshȧ*), through equating the O.K. title with the later as *mr mšʿ*; but an examination of the former shows that the equation is wrong:—

, L., *D.*, ii., 43, *c*, *d*, *mr mšʿ nfrw*, "director of the marching of recruits," corresponds exactly to , L., *D.*, ii., 97, *a*, *mr mšʿ šs*, "director of the marching of trained soldiers," and although the writing of the latter title varies greatly (*Medum*, ix.; L., *D.*, ii., 21, 22) down to (*Mon. div.*, Pl. xx.), the three elements can always be distinguished, and , (cf. *Una*, l. 25, for the same spelling independently of the title) is evidently a separate word, viz. *šs*. Both of these titles disappeared very early, probably at the end of the IVth Dynasty.

C. HUMAN ACTION.

Fig. 163. Man standing, raising his hands on either side of his head.

Regular det., and occasionally word-sign for *ḥʿʿ* (*ḥȧȧ*), "rejoice," and after O.K. for *q'* (*qa*), "high"; for either of these it may stand as ab. (PETRIE, *T. el A.*, xxii., 13; *Kah. Pap.*, xiv., l. 33).

Fig. 34. Man building a rectangular enclosure with battlements.

Word-sign for *qd*, "build," not used in O.K., at which time, however, the enclosure by itself is det. of the word, and sometimes has the form (*Pyr. M.*, l. 566, &c.), but generally is a rectangle of varying breadth (*N.* 1174; *Methen*, L., *D.*, ii., 7, *b*).

[*B. H.*, iii., fig. 54.] Arms held downwards, with or without vase, corn-rubber, or other object which they are taking or holding.

Word-sign for *sẖn* (*sekhen*), and *pg'* (*pega*), "embrace," "comprehend," &c., with phon. trans.; also det. of *ḥpt*, *ynq* (*ȧnq*), which have a similar meaning.

Fig. 165; *B. H.*, iii., fig. 43. (*q.v.*) between the two arms held downwards. In O.K. the arms are held more squarely.

Graphic compound denoting *ḥn k'* (*ḥen ka*), "*ka*-servant," or "*ka*-priest." The second element is the usual form of *k'* in this compound group, probably because it would have been considered irreverent to place the sign for "servant" above that for the *ka*, though also is found. So also in the earliest inscriptions we have , but when compounded with for "the spiritualized *ka*," it is turned downwards (De Morgan, *Recherches*, ii., p. 240, figs. 802 and 806).

The sign is phon. for $k^{\text{ʾ}}$ (*ka*).

Much has been said on the *ka* of Egyptian religious belief, but I am not aware that any explanation of the sign by which its name is written has been attempted. If, as seems probable, the sign was intended to represent the *ka* symbolically, and not merely phonetically, one may perhaps believe that the latter was, from one point of view, regarded as the source of muscular movement and power, as opposed to *ba*, the will or soul which set it in motion. The human arms, hands, and fingers are the members of the body which carry out the most intelligent and intricate promptings of will and desire, and produce the most surprising results. They might therefore well be chosen to represent the muscular life, the energy and activity of man. On the other hand, they might be considered as held up, , to receive life from the sun, and offerings after death, and downwards, , to receive the service of the *ḥen-ka*. But this seems less probable. The word , *k*ʾ·*t* (*ka·t*), "labours," "handiwork," is not improbably from the same root; and may be the origin of the value for the sign (see).

Fig. 177. Human arms holding shield and mace; the form of the shield varies in different instances (*Medum*, Pl. xii., L., *D.*, ii., 97*a*, &c.). The printed type shows a halberd or war axe for the mace.

Word-symbol (but not det.) of fighting, = "fight," with rad. ext. In *Pyr.* we have , *N.*, l. 689 = , *M.*, l. 179 = , *T.*, l. 170. In M.K. changed to , as usual before (see p. 5), *Horhotep*, l. 104 = l. 529 (*Todt.*, cap. 17). The proper name *Yḥ*ʾ (*Âḥa*) is apparently the alphabetic spelling of , e.g. *El B.*, ii., tomb 8, p. 38, and Pl. xxi., though it does not actually vary with it. In XXVIth Dyn. we have (for *yḥ*ʾ) (Mar., *M. D.*, xc. b.), which, from the context, is certainly the verb *yḥ*ʾ, "fight," and not *ḥw*, "strike."

Fig. 68. Two arms grasping a paddle, as in paddling, issuing from an object shaped like , but in M.K. more like (hollow).

Word-sign for "paddling," . No early variants of the sign are known, but a few very late ones give *ḫn* (*khen*), and this is probably accurate, since it never occurs in the name of the *m·ḫn·t* boat, and there is already the semi-phon. for *ḫn* (*chen*). The use of is confined to a few words, and it is hardly a phon. The (?) *ḫ*ʾ (*kha*) may be an indication of its phonetic value.

[*B. H.*, iii., fig. 50.] Arm, or two arms, , holding magic wand named *mkś*, or *nḫb·t*; for which see *Mentuhotep*, p. 18, no. 7, and *Pyr.*

Word-sign for *zśr*, "sacred," &c. (*Pyr. P.*, l. 121 = *T.*, l. 175), the sign indicating that what is evil and profane is warded off. Used with rad. ext.

Fig. 122. Human arm, the hand holding a short stick.

This sign is found (probably not till after O.K.) as det. of strength and of actions demanding strength. In N.K. it occasionally is word-sign for *nḫt* (*nekht*), "strength" (Budge, *Bk. of D.*, p. 11, l. 1), and so it agrees in use almost precisely with .

Fig. 64. A human arm; in the open hand a cake or other mass of material.

From O.K. onwards this is the word-sign for the verb , , also written *m*, which is found only in the imperative *m*, e.g. *Pyr.*, *N.*, l. 660, and as an optative with suffixes *m·k*, *m·tn*, having the force of the English "Behold"—thou (or ye) a certain thing in a certain state. One might be disposed to connect its meaning with the of , more correctly , *ym* (*ȧm*), "give," "place," and of , *my* (*mȧ*), "Come!" &c. We should then suppose it to indicate "giving," "placing," like the graphic compound , *dy* (*dȧ*), "place" (see , below), with which it is often confused in print, especially as (which is really *ḥnk*, "present") sometimes stands for .

But in *Paheri*, Pl. iv., top middle, the sign figures as det. of , *šsp* (*shesep*), "receive." The idea in seems thus to be of "receiving" rather than "giving," "placing," , while can symbolize apparently either "receiving," *m*, or "offering to deities," *ḥnk*. Hence expressions like , *m·k wy y·kwy*, "Behold thou me, I am arrived," i.e. "Behold, I am come!" literally mean something like, "Receive me, I am come," "receive" having here the sense "perceive," "behold" (*v.* Addenda).

After O.K. is often written or , with det. , or alone; and , whether formative or otherwise, at the beginning of words, is very frequently written with (in some texts) or its equivalent . Cf. Erm., *Gram.*, §§ 35, 102, 256.

Fig. 156. A pair of human "feet," (*q.v.*), joined at the top and striding.

Word-sign for the common verb "travel," "step," "come," which varies with in the name of the goddess *Iw·s-ȧa·s* (*Pyr. P.*, l. 423 = *N.*, l. 1210), and therefore reads *yw* (*ȧu*). , apparently *yw·wt*, is a not uncommon expression for "movements" and "visits." Also det. of all words of motion.

A number of verbs of motion are written by compounding this sign with their principal consonant, e.g. = *šm* (*shem*), "go" (used also by rad. ext.); = *ytt* (*ȧtheth*), "take," "seize" (used also as phon. for *tt* in *btt*, "colic?"); = *s*, "pass (?)" (*Pyr. N.* 1002 = *M.* 604); *sb*, "conduct" (used also as phon. in *msb*, "offer"); and = *y*(*ȧ*), "come," &c.; or with their word-sign, e.g. *šmš*, "follow," *sšm*, "conduct."

[*B. H.*, iii., fig. 94.] Vase on a pair of human "feet" (*v.*); in O.K. the shanks are thick in proportion to their length. To give prominence to the they are closer together than in , but are otherwise identical with .

Word-sign for *yn* (*ȧn*), "carry," with rad. ext.; probably enters into it as forming a good picture-compound with , the det. of motion, and as supplying approximately the phonetic value by its own value *n*(*w*).

D. Mammals and Parts of Mammals.

Figs. 91, 93. Forepart of lion, showing head, shoulder, and foreleg.

The name of this portion of an animal's body is , *ḥ*ᶜ*·t* (*ḥȧ·t*), "front part," and thence it has, by phon. trans., the value of *ḥ*ᶜ, occasionally changing to *ḥ*ʾ (*ḥa*) (see p. 5): e.g. in *ḥ*ᶜ*·tï*, "heart," in M.K. sometimes *ḥ*ʾ*·tï*, *v.* .

The title , in spite of its spelling, is an ab., and ought to be read *ḥ*ᶜ*·ti* (*ḥȧ·ti*), "he who is at the front," "leader," "dux"—derived from the above *ḥ*ᶜ*·t*. This is pretty clearly proved by N.K. texts; and in early times the fem. is written , *ḥ*ᶜ*·tt*, corresponding to a masc. *ḥ*ᶜ*·ti*.

Fig. 2. The desert hare (*Lepus aegyptiaca*), common in Egypt; the length and size of its ears are always absurdly exaggerated in Egyptian drawing. In fig. 175 the ears are more preposterous even than usual.

In the tombs of Beni Hasan the hare is called *sḫ*ᶜ*·t* (*sechȧ·t*). But in *Ptahhetep*, Pl. xxxii., and elsewhere, , *wn* (*un*), "run," "bound along swiftly" (det., outstretched legs joined at thighs), suggests that it was once called "the swift runner," or at any rate that it symbolized such motion.

Common phon. for *wn* (*un*), especially after O.K.

Fig. 175. The hare as a sacred badge raised on the sacred perch (*q.v.*, p. 58), with food as usual, planted in the symbol of a nome.

The nome-sign of the XVth nome of Upper Egypt (Hermopolis Magna); compare that of the XVIth nome, *B. H.*, iii., frontispiece, and p. 6. It is difficult to ascertain the reading of this class of symbols. The nome-signs appear to be of the feminine gender, for the qualifying adjectives *ḫnt·t*, "upper," and *pḥ·t*, "lower," which occur with several of them, are fem. in inscriptions of good period (see *Ptahhetep*, Pl. xxxv., for XXth-XXIst nomes, and *Siut*, Tomb iii., l. 21, for XIIIth nome of Upper Egypt). The present symbol also is often written , with fem. termination in the early M.K. (*El B.*, ii., xiii. 2; *Hetnub Graffiti*, viii., l. 1, ix., l. 1, &c.; cf. *Siut*, Tomb iv., l. 36, i., l. 151). The badge itself, may have its usual value *wn* (see above), especially as the nome capital was named , *Wnw* (*Unu*) (see *Hetnub Graffiti*, i., l. 7, viii., l. 11); and the whole nome-sign may thus read *Wn·t* (*Un·t*). It is almost certain that has no separate value in this sign (*v.*).

[*B. H.*, iii., fig. 35.] Ram with horizontal horns. Similar animals are shown in the earliest sculptures (*Naqada*, Pl. lxxvii., top right; De Morgan, *Recherches*, ii., Pl. iii.), but it is difficult to say whether they represent sheep or goats. (The variety of sheep with curved horns, which superseded this kind, was the animal of Amen, probably first consecrated to him in N.K.; as the sacred ram it was called *rhni.*)

Its name is *sr*, ⲉⲥⲟⲟⲩ, "sheep," in the tomb of Renni at El Kab, where it is distinguished from the goats (C., *Mons.*, ii., Pl. cxlii., 3). It was sacred to Chnem, and is det. of his name. At Mendes it was sacred to Osiris under the name of , meaning "soul"; or perhaps, with reference to the employment of rams in agriculture (L., *D.*, ii., 106*b*), really "plougher," *v.* , but this does not seem to be otherwise a name for the ram.

Fig. 48; *B. H.*, iii., fig. 31. An indeterminate-looking animal newly dropped, in fig. 48 having some of the features of an ass's foal, but with sprouting horns. As Borchardt remarks, it can hardly be a calf; possibly a kid was intended as the type.

Phon. for *yw* (*àu*) in the O.K. and onwards. As the word *ywr* (*àur*), "conceive," generally , is sometimes written in *Pyr.* (*M.* 466), it is clear that this sign has an affinity to *yw*[*r*] with weak *r*; cf. also *Kah. Pap.*, p. 11, for further evidence of this. may thus be taken as "the conceived thing," "embryo (?)," properly written *yw*[*r*], but used regularly for *yw*. Cf. for a very similar case. It is possible that it has also a word-sign value *yʿ*, the root of the word for "heirship," "inheritance," &c.; cf. *Pyr. M.*, l. 760, "heir." But an occasional variant, , indicates that the reading in this case is really *ywʿ* (*àuà*), the "foal" having its ordinary value (*yw*) as phon.; and this is the opinion of the best authorities.

[*B. H.*, iii., fig. 55.] Shoulder and foreleg of an animal.

Word-sign for *ḫpš* (*khepsh*), "shoulder" (as a joint of meat), "strength of arm." In N.K. the name of the scimetar, , from its shape; later, a word for the human arms, as in Coptic ϣⲟⲡϣ (*Sign Pap.*, *passim*). It seems never to mean "the haunch," though in the printed sign the jointing corresponds to that of the hind leg.

 Fig. 121. This sign, resembling a spiked club in outline, at Medum is coloured black and white, most of the "head" being white. PETRIE (*Medum*, p. 30) pointed out that the projections are clearly mammae, and that the sign represents the teats and other sexual parts on the belly of an animal.

The word for "belly," "loins," "womb," is  *ḥ·t* (*chet*), and this is evidently the origin of the alphabetic value *ḥ*. constantly varies with  in O.K., while  does so only very rarely. The distinction between  and was pointed out by Steindorff very recently, and it is found that the two signs are seldom confused until a very late period.

 Fig. 155. A rib bone, in the present example (*El B.*, i., Pl. xviii., 1) very clearly represented. Often identical in form with the lip, *šp·t*.

The name of the rib is 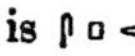 *špr*. Used with phon. trans. (usually accompanied by the alph. complement  *r*).

 **Fig. 192.** The haunch or shoulder, trimmed and shrunk by boiling.

This joint was of two kinds, called in the tables of offerings respectively 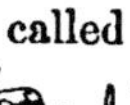, 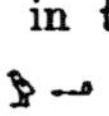 or  *yw*ʿ or *y*ʿ (*àuà* or *àà*), and ,  *šw·t* (*šut*), perhaps with radical *t*; one is probably the shoulder, the other the fore-leg (cf. in N.K.  () 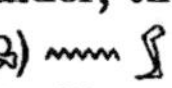 "*snt* of the fore-leg (?)," *Leyd. Mon.*, iii., Pl. xxiv.).

With the value of the former name it is transferred to other meanings, and is then written with the alph. complement . In  it is also word-sign for 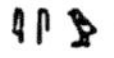 *yšw* (*àšu*), "reward," "price." From *Siut*, Tomb i., l. 276, it seems possible that when an ox was given for sacrifice, the *àuà*-joint was customarily set apart for the special benefit of the donor—hence, or perhaps for some similar reason, the signification "reward."

 **Figs. 46, 166.** A conventional picture of the heart with arteries; the vessels at top and sides trimmed short; in the first example, the paler colouring of the upper part of the heart itself seems to indicate a covering of fat. Fig. 166 is a very common type: the markings upon it may indicate conventionally the interior structure as displayed in section. Cf. *Medum*, Pl. xiii., and the lute (?), .

The heart, 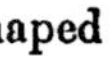, must be distinguished from the heart-shaped vase, which, being a characteristic form in granite, is word-sign and det. of  *m'ṯ* (*math*), "granite."

Word-sign for  *yb* (*àb*), "heart," "desire," &c. (*Pyr. W.*, l. 451 = *T.*, l. 259). Det. of 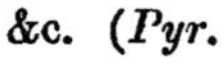, in M.K. sometimes , *ḥ*ʿ*ti*, *ḥ'ti* (*ḥàti*, *ḥati*), another word for "heart."

 **Fig. 47.** A difficult sign to explain, but probably representing in a conventional manner some internal portion of mammalian anatomy—such as a pair of glands and the duct belonging to them—the kidneys or the liver (?).

Word-sign for 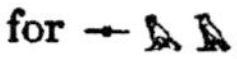, 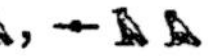 *sm'*, *s'm* (*sma*, *sam*), generally with the meaning "unite."  is the name of the kidneys (?), with perhaps the liver; and  in *Pap. Eb.* is "colon" (?), "liver" (?), and in *Pyr.* the plural (*W.*, l. 518; *T.*, l. 328) stands for kidneys (so Maspero), with perhaps the liver and other edible portions of the viscera; and 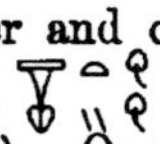 *sm'·ti* (dual) in *Pap. Eb.* is "testiculi" (?). One or other of these two words must be the origin of the phonetic value.

 [*B. H.*, iii., fig. 46.] Hide of domestic animal, stripped off and wrapped together. In *Deshasheh*, Pl. xxv., it is shown tightly twisted, with a peg through one end, perhaps with reference to the common meaning "pull," "strain," of the word-sign.

Word-sign for šd, "pull," "strip off," and for šd·w, "water-skin," which in *Deshasheh*, Pl. xix., is very clearly shown by its det.; the last use suggests that šd, "dragged off," is one name for a hide. Also phon. for šd. Loret has studied the sign and its uses, *Rec. de Trav.*, xi., pp. 117-131 (*v.* Addenda).

Cf. **Fig. 167.** Hide of wild animal.
Word-sign for ʾb (*ab*) from the earliest times (De Morgan, *Recherches*, ii., fig. 786); it may be connected with the much-prized hide of the leopard, the name of that animal being . Max Müller thinks it the origin of the phon. = ʾb, *Rec. de trav.*, ix., 159.
Det. of hide, names of animals, &c.

Fig. 167. A hide—perhaps hung as a target—pierced by an arrow or dart.
In O.K. word-sign for , apparently šṯt (*sethet*), "shoot," "throw," and probably equivalent to šṯt (written with , *Pyr. W.*, l. 422; *T.*, l. 242), "engender" (cf. *B. H.*, ii., Pl. iv., top row, left). Later it stands for allied words—št, "sprinkle" (which is perhaps only a simplified form of šṯt, reduplicated being sometimes)—and others with value st, and is completely interchangeable with .

E. Birds and their Parts.

Figs. 4, 73, 120; *B. H.*, iii., fig. 13. It is very satisfactory to be able to illustrate this bird and the eagle by such decisive examples as figs. 1 and 4. Their outlines are often very similar in inferior writing, and copyists generally confound them, but in hieratic the two birds are always distinguished, and generally in linear hieroglyphs. This bird is the Egyptian vulture (*Neophron percnopterus*). In early examples the colouring of the wing is grey or blue. Later it is green, probably owing to the use of a compound colour from which the vegetable element has disappeared; it has been remarked that the green may have been mixed with pink madder (used in Roman times, cf. Russell in *Medum*, p. 47) in order to obtain a grey. The flesh at the base of the bill is naked, and the scanty feathering beyond often makes the neck appear thin; in O.K. drawing this long sparse feathering appears as a kind of crest (see *Medum*, Pl. xiv., and *Methen*, L., *D.*, ii., 6). These characteristics, and the weak bill combined with the short neck, determine the species absolutely.

The name of the bird and the origin of its alphabetic value ʾ, i.e. *alif* (conventionally *a*), are unknown.

Fig. 76. A bird of raptorial aspect, but with two small tufts at the back of the head and a longer tuft on the neck. There is no original colour left on the example figured; good examples of this curious bird-hieroglyph are much needed. In early instances the head-tufts are absent, but an additional tuft sometimes hangs like a beard or wattle from the base of the beak, and often the form is almost that of the chick , with one or more tufts. Probably it will prove to be not raptorial.

Name, , nḥ, in *Todt.*, cliii. B. (Budge, 397, l. 12, cf. Nav., i., Pl. clxxviii., l. 13). Phon. for nḥ.

Figs. 1, 75. A brown raptorial bird, having fully feathered neck and strong beak. In the fine example, fig. 1, it must be an eagle In fig. 75 the form is less distinctive. In *Medum*, frontispiece, figs. 1, 3, the appearance is very different, but may still be an unsatisfactory rendering of the eagle.

The sign has the value tiw (*tiu*) as a grammatical termination, this being the plural ending of adjectives in ti derived from fem. substantives in t. The origin of this value is at present obscure.

 [cf. *B. H.*, iii., fig. 5.] Sparrow-hawk; a male bird, fairly well represented in form and colour.

Det. of, but apparently never word-sign for, its name 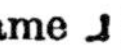 *byk* (*bâk*). Word-sign for 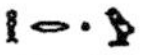 *Ḥr·w* (the god "Horus"), lit. "the soarer," "he who flies up" (See , the hawk-perch).

 [*B. H.*, iii., 5.] Graphic compound of  and the sparrow-hawk.

Word-sign for 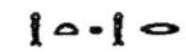 *Ḥt-Ḥr* (Hathor). Professor Maspero considers that the literal meaning "House of Horus" is not to be insisted on, and that the compound is merely an attempt to spell the name of the goddess phonetically.

 **Figs. 7, 183, 185**; *B. H.*, iii., fig. 7. Owl; the type varies but is not long-eared until very late times.

To account for the alphabetic value *m* it may be suggested that the Coptic name ⲙⲟⲩⲗⲁϫ is possibly a compound, of which the first element, *m* (?), represents the ancient name. Note the owl-names in Ar. *bûm*, in Latin *bubo*, from which it would appear that *m* would be onomatopoeic. A very curious use of the sign occurs in *Pyr.*, where it stands as det. for  *ḥśq*, "chop off" the head or limbs, in *N.*, l. 904; while in *M.*, l. 26, &c.,  is the symbol for the same word. Perhaps this points to the owl being a bird of ill-omen, which it was desirable to behead when caught.

 **Figs. 3, 99**; *B. H.*, iii., figs. 9, 14. Swallow: to include under this term perhaps martins and swifts (*Cypselus*). The general outline and broad, slightly forked, tail are constant, but colour and markings vary considerably. (*a*) In the earliest examples (*Medum*, frontispiece, fig. 4; *B. H.*, iii., fig. 9, Ameny) it is grey, with white belly and a black spot on breast, though in *Medum* the latter is often absent (cf. *Chelidon urbica*). (*b*) Later, green is substituted for grey—as in the case of the Egyptian vulture—and the breast marking disappears (see *B. H.*, iii., fig. 14, Chnemhetep, and below, fig. 99). (*c*) In the present instance the green remains, but the under parts are flushed with orange. The form (*a*) seems to represent the sand martin (*Cotyle riparia*); without the dark mark it may be the common martin (*C. urbica*). The substitution of green for grey in (*b*) is apparently of no specific significance. An orange or rufous tinge on the under parts, as in (*c*), is found in some swallows.

The true swallow (*Hirundo rustica*) and its congeners are named 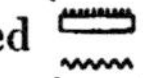,  *mn·t*, and are pictured in the vignette of *Todt.*, cap. 86, sometimes with true swallow tail, at others (*Pap. Bul.*, iii., Pl. 21) with that of the martin. The latter form is well shown on a stele figured in MASPERO, *Premières Mêlées*, p. 536; LANZ., *Diz. d. Mit.*, Pl. cxviii.

The sign is, however, phon. for  *wr*—which as a word means "great," "old,"—and it is supposed that a bird 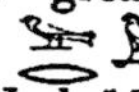 *wr* (with det. of deity) occurs in *Pyr. N.*, l. 157. LORET, *Ä. Z.*, 1892, p. 28, quotes this group in connexion with , and identifies the bird—if bird it be, and not merely "the great (deity)"—with the Coptic ⲟⲩⲗⲁ, ⲃⲗⲁ, which in a compound word seems to mean "domestic pigeon," i.e. the rock-dove (*Columba livia*, not *C. oenas*, as has been stated, cf. SHELLEY, *Birds*, p. 211). His explanation seems possible, for in *Ptahhetep*, Pl. xli., third row of offerings (= DÜM., *Res.*, Pl. xiii.), the name of the pigeon, 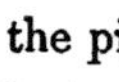, 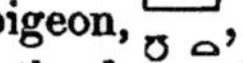 *mnw·t* (*menu·t*), is apparently determined by a bird of  outline.  does not, however, in the least resemble the pictures of pigeons in *Ptahhetep*, Pls. xxxi., xxxvii., and *B. H.*, i., Pl. xxx.; and it is not improbable that the  figure in *Ptahhetep* is a slight mistake of the sculptor, due also in part to the close similarity of the names *mnw·t*, "pigeon," and *mn·t*, "swallow" (*v.* Addenda).

Figs. 5, 189; *B. H.*, iii., fig. 15. Chick of a gallinaceous bird.

The chick referred to in *B. H.*, iii., p. 8, as figured in *Ptahhetep*, apparently for the typical quail of the farmyard, appears in Pl. xxxi. of the new publication of that tomb. Probably the eggs of quail (and occasionally partridge), found abundantly in the harvest field, were hatched artificially in the farmyard, and thus the chicks were familiar objects. Quail flying over a cornfield are very well rendered in the tomb of Khaemha (PRISSE, *Art*, ii., 11 = *Mons.*, Pl. xl.). The sign is perhaps not without significance too in connexion with the peculiar form of the adult bird. The alphabetic value *w* (*u*) for is perhaps onomatopoeic.

Fig. 28. An unfledged bird with open mouth, eager to be fed; as often represented in nests in paintings of the N.K.

The name for a chick either in the shell or just hatched is , *t'* (*tha*); cf. BREASTED *De Hymnis*, p. 44. The meaning of the name is probably "taker" (from "take"), owing to the eagerness of the nestling to take its food. See the fine outline in *Medum*, Pl. xxi., which is very suggestive of this meaning. Phon. for .

Fig. 74; *B. H.*, iii., figs. 3, 10. A bird of the type of the *Grallatores*, with tuft on breast. In O.K. generally without the tuft (*Medum*, Pl. xxi.; *Ptahhetep*, Pl. xli., fourth row of offerings). This type may have been suggested in a general way by plover, ibis, crane, or snipe, but does not agree with any particular species. It reminds one also of the bustards.

Name unknown. Word-sign for *b'* (*ba*) meaning, amongst other things, "soul" (*v.*), and "hoe," "break up earth," sometimes written . We may best connect its value with the habit of the plover tribe (as well as of the crane) of digging their bills into the ground or ooze in search of food in the newly-sown corn-fields; , in fact, in *Pyr.* is occasionally word-sign for *b'* (*ba*), "soul," see SCHACK, *Index*. is also phon. for *b'*, most commonly spelt . In the stereotyped group (once , SH., *Eg. Ins.*, ii., 22, l. 10, from Louvre, C., ii.), "servant," "serve," "work," there is no need to assign a special value, *bk*, to the sign; it is, as usual, simply *b'*. As in so many cases, the *b'* changed to *b* in the N.K., hence the rare N.K. spelling *bk*, *Rec. de Trav.*, v., 74.

Cf. Fig. 168. Sacred ibis (*Ibis religiosa*), white, with black unfeathered skin on head and neck, black legs (and tail). The bird of Thoth.

Name, *hb*, lit. "plougher," cf. "plough," *Pyr. P.*, l. 763 = , *M.*, l. 764.

Fig. 168. "Sacred" ibis on sacred perch, (*q.v.*, p. 58); the usual food held in place by a peg (other food (?) beneath its feet), cf. *Medum*, Pl. xxi.

Emblem of the XVth nome of Lower Egypt, the name of which was apparently *Zhw't* (*Zhu't*). Hence must be derived the well-known name of the nome-god , (*Kahun*, Pl. v.; *El B.*, ii., &c.) *Zhw'ti*, "Thoth," lit. "the Zehutian"; compare Osiris called *Ånz'ti*, "he of Anzet," from the IXth nome of Lower Egypt.

Fig. 118; *B. H.*, iii., fig. 4. Crested ibis (*Ibis comata*). This bird is glossy purple, with naked red flesh on head. It is now found in South Algeria and across Abyssinia into Arabia (HEUGLIN, *Ornithologie*, p. 1144). It has apparently never been recorded from Egypt, but there is no other bird with which the type can be identified.

The value as a word-sign, *y'ḫ* (*åakh*)—or perhaps *'ḫ* only—with phon. transf., is given by *Pyr. W.*, l. 590, by variants quoted in Br., *Wtb.*, and by the variation with *y'ḥ* in later times. If this was the name of the bird, it probably means "the glossy." The radical idea of *y'ḥ* may be that of red light, like the light of the rising or setting sun (cf. , *y'ḥ·t* (*ȧakh·t*), "the place of sunrise or sunset"); but it refers especially to the glorified state of the dead in heaven, as spirits illuminated by the sun (cf. the quotation below, *s.v.*). In a few passages of the *Todt.*, the "glorified spirit," appears as something parallel to the (*ba*), and the (*ka*), as if it might be, like them, a distinct part of the human organism. But such instances are extremely rare. In the *Lebensmüder* I read it that the man is not conversing with his , but with his (*ba*), "soul"; for *b'* in hieratic see *Ä. T.*, xvii., l. 40.

In late Egyptian and in Coptic the word is used for "ghost," "demon," with no suggestion of blessedness, but the reverse.

Fig. 97. White plumeless egret (*Ardea*), with fish, (represented with the present value in various attitudes seizing or swallowing the fish; cf. *Ptahhetep*, Pl. xli., fourth row of offerings; *Paheri*, Pl. iv.; L., *D.*, ii., 70, heron (?) with plumes).

Word-sign for *ḥ'm* (*ḥam*), later *ḥm*, "catch fish." The pelican in Coptic is named "the fisher," ϩⲁⲙ (masc.), ϩⲁⲙⲓ (fem.).

Fig. 79. The flamingo (*Phoenicopterus antiquorum*), characteristically portrayed in *Medum*, frontispiece, fig. 6.

The name of the bird, *dšr* (*deshe̱r*), is preserved in the late text of Leps., *Todt.*, cap. xxxi., l. 9, unfortunately not found in the earlier papyri. It means "the ruddy," and by rad. ext. the sign is used for all other words derived from the same root.

[*B. H.*, iii., fig. 6.] Wild goose; evidently *Anser albifrons* in spring plumage, though the colouring of the head is inaccurate.

In L., *D.*, ii., 61*b*, the bird is figured, with its name , as the first—thus suggesting that it was the largest—of all the geese there; but it is rarely shown as domesticated. It is the wild goose , *gb'w*, of *Pap. Har.* (500 *verso*, p. xii., ll. 7, 9); it is perhaps also the of *Pap. Eb.* The name of the god , Greek Κηβ, varies with *gb*, *gbb'* (*gebba*), &c., see Brugsch, *Ä. Z.*, 1886, p. 1; Spiegelberg, *Rec. de Trav.*, xvii., 94. As a word-sign the goose is always distinguished by the complement . In form it is probably often confused with the duck of fig. 11.

[*B. H.*, iii., fig. 12.] In spite of its rather short neck, apparently a white-fronted goose, in pale winter plumage, and domesticated.

Word-sign for *ḥtm*, written , generally meaning "supply," "fill," and "destroy." "Supply," "completeness," is perhaps the idea here indicated by the fat goose ready for killing. How far the species is constant in the early hieroglyphs it is as yet impossible to say. In *El B.*, i., Pl. xxv., the outline resembles that of the pin-tail duck, which likewise was domesticated and fattened.

In *B. H.*, iii., p. 8, the name of the material was read *ḥs'*; but the spelling of the name is constant, the only variant being (Düm., *Peduamenap*, Pl. xx., no. 27), so there can be no doubt that it reads *ḥtm*.

Fig. 11. A brightly coloured duck with two long feathers in the tail: the latter peculiarity is copied from the pin-tail duck (*Dafila acuta*). The colouring, however, is much exaggerated, evidently as a general distinction of ducks from geese.

This example (fig. 11) stands for the word

"son," s. In *Pyr.* we have the word for "son" written , that for "daughter" . In *Medum*, Pl. xiii., by exception the colouring of the bird is more sober, and thus more like that of the pin-tail. The domesticated duck, named *s·t*, which, like the small *ser*-duck, is never absent from scenes of the poultry-farm, has the two long central tail-feathers of the pin-tail, e.g. in *Ptahhetep*, Pl. xxxvii. It is thus clear that the *Dafila acuta*, which abounds in Lower Egypt (SHELLEY, *Birds*, p. 284), is the Egyptian type of a large duck, and was regularly domesticated. To all appearance it is also identical with the phon. for *s*ʾ (*sa*), and if so, its name is no doubt from a root *s*ʾ, perhaps *s*ʾ, "keep" (cf. *šb*, from root *šb*ʾ, p. 30).

Goose and duck being closely similar in outline, are generally written with phonetic complements to distinguish them, thus: *s*ʾ; *gb*; *ḥtm*. The principal exceptions to this rule are , "son," and "daughter."

[*B. H.*, iii., figs. 1, 8.] Flying duck (pin-tail, *Dafila acuta*).

Word-sign for *p*ʾ (*pa*), "fly," and phon. for *p*ʾ.

[*B. H.*, iii., fig. 11; *B. H.*, i., Pl. xxvii.]. Duck, fed to repletion. In both instances the type is the same, but it is difficult to fix the species; perhaps the widgeon (*Mareca penelope*) is intended.

Word-sign for *wš*ʾ (*usha*), "feed by cramming" (*B. H.*, i., Pl. xxvii.; cf. L., *D.*, ii., 62, fourth row, and 102*b*). The reading in the group , *B. H.*, iii., p. 7, is uncertain; perhaps it is *zf*ʾ (*zefa*), a word for rich food (fatlings?), which in N.K. has this sign for det.

[Cf. *B. H.*, iii., fig. 29.] Goose or duck plucked.

Word-sign for *šnz*, "fear," "helpless fear"; probably due to the practice of plucking geese, &c., alive, the feathers being then more easily removed. Det. of *wšn* (*ushen*), "prepare birds for table."

Fig. 150. The head and neck of duck (as here) or goose is a frequent ab. for the whole bird as det. at all periods. In the present instance the sign probably accompanied (destroyed) as part of det. of "offerings." In *Ptahhetep*, Pl. xxxix., table of offerings, different sorts of geese are represented by a phonetic indicator, followed by det. of a goose's head, viz. "*r*-goose," "*trp*-goose."

[*B. H.*, iii., fig. 72.] Feather (of ostrich?). Word-sign for *šw·t*, "feather," with rad. ext., having such meanings as "desert-waste," "shadow," "empty," the god *Shu*, i.e. "empty space" the first-born of the Sun, &c.

Word-sign for the name of the goddess of Truth, *m*ˣ*·t* (*Maā·t*), "the true" or "just," with phon. trans. The connexion between the feather and truth or justice may partly be suggested by the feathering of an arrow, which allows it to fly "straight." The just man is said to act "not leaning to one side." The lightness of a feather, which would not materially affect the weight in a rude and primitive balance, might also be held as symbolic of justice, that will not introduce personal bias into a question (*v.* also).

F. REPTILES, FISHES, INSECTS, SHELLS, &C.

Fig. 83; *B. H.*, iii., figs. 102, 103. Piece of crocodile-skin, from the tail, with spines; or in the third example, of fish-skin with spines, from the back of the fish. This is apparently the "crocodile's tail" of *Horapollo*, i., 70. According to Borchardt, a suggestion of Schäfer's that the sign represents a heap of charcoal from which flames issue, is confirmed by the ancient examples. This explanation would account for the meaning "black," *km*, but it is not confirmed by our facsimiles.

Word-sign for *km*, probably not used as phon. There is a word , var. *ykm* (*åkem*), meaning "shield," which occurs constantly on M.K. coffins, &c. Not improbably the crocodile plates, or fish scales, , were known by the same name, *ykm* (*åkem*), "shield." This would account for the value *km*. Cf. *ybḥ* (*åbeḥ*), "tooth," giving to the value *bḥ*.

[*B. H.*, iii., fig. 24.] Green lizard.

The name of the lizard is (...) *ḥnt'*, or more fully, *ḥnt'š'w*.

Word-sign for *'š'* (*åsha*), "numerous," presumably from the numbers in which it was found anciently.

Figs. 16, 173. A snake, often with green band below the throat.

Word-sign for *z·t*, "serpent," written , in *Pyr. N.*, ll. 703, 955, &c, which perhaps stands for the *Echis* or viper, in contradistinction to the uraeus. By phon. trans. used also as word-sign for the "body," , , "eternity," &c.

Alph. for *z*.

The group (in which fig 16 occurs) is ab. for , *zd mdw*, "say words."

Figs. 35, 151; *B. H.*, iii., fig. 69. Cerastes (?). Slug (?). This animal, according to PRISSE, *Mons.*, ii., Pl. 62 (reproduced in *B. H.*, iii., p. 23), was capable of creeping up the stem of a water-plant, and should therefore be a slug —to which animal it bears considerable resemblance—or perhaps a snail represented as without its shell. But it also resembles in many points the cerastes, with the "horns" immensely exaggerated, and in the vignettes of *Todt.*, cap. 150 (*Nebseny*), it varies with a hornless snake. In the Gnostic papyrus of Leyden (p. xvii., l. 27) of about the second century A.D., the "gall," *sḫy* (*sekhy*) of a *fy* (with det. or) is prescribed, and this cannot apply to a slug, which has no gall. It is therefore certain that at that time the *fy*, no doubt our *f*, was considered to be a cerastes. Borchardt states that on the coffin of Antef (M.K.) at Berlin, the is regularly figured with a forked tongue; so here again we have the cerastes.

It seems, therefore, that the after all represents the cerastes, and that the Theban artist (PRISSE, *Mons.*, ii., Pl. 62), seeing a slug ascending a stem, noted its resemblance to the , and drew it in the manner prescribed for that. Perhaps a confusion between the slug and the cerastes led to Herodotus' account (ii., 74) of a small, harmless, two-horned serpent, which was sacred to Zeus (Amen) at Thebes. A slug, *Arion ater*, is recorded from Egypt, according to Mr. Edgar Smith of the British Museum. In ancient times it may have been more common in the gardens of great houses and in the marshy lands.

From the earliest period we meet with , probably "rock or mount of the ," as the name of the XIIth nome of Upper Egypt. This expression implies a serpent rather than a slug. Opposite the nome of , on the east of the Nile, lay the XIIIth, that of , on the west of the river, and beyond this the XIVth, which was of the same name. Late inscriptions indicate that the reading of is *'tf* (*atef*), or perhaps *ytf* (*åtef*) (see BR., *D. G.*, p. 6). But probably, on the analogy of , we should divide this into *'t·f* (*at·f*), and the ancient reading may have been "Perch (?) of the ," like , which probably means "Perch (?) of the ," i.e. the griffon vulture (*Pyr. T.*, l. 76). appears also in the late hieroglyphs , "go out," "enter."

Alph. for *f*. Especially common as representing the suffix of third pers. sing. masc. This value may be derived from *fy*, the name of the cerastes, but as the name *fy* occurs only in the latest period, that name may be only a late derivative from the *f* value.

In the common groups , , reading *yt* (*àt*), "father," and found from the earliest times as variants of , (Erm., *Gram.*, § 31), the may be considered as the suffix *f*, used redundantly for some cause or other, perhaps to give the word a more distinctive appearance. On the other hand, it may be regarded as a true id. or det., possibly from some superstition connected with the cerastes or slug. In N.K. the plural of the word is often "fathers." There is also a variant , *yt ntr* (*àt neter*), "divine father," as the name or description of a kind of clothing (*Pyr. M.*, l. 118; *P.*, l. 94), for (*N.*, l. 57), which thus indicates that may sometimes actually be read *yt* (*àt*). Perhaps , the "*fy* (?) serpent," represented *yt* (*àt*), "father," just as , the *ner*-vulture (see above) represented , *m·t*, "mother."

One may perhaps derive the phon. value *f* for from the suffix of the third pers. sing. masc., *f*, supposing the symbol for "father" to be taken as representative of "he," "his." Cf. = *św*, p. 29, and = *ś*, p. 45.

Fig. 98. The *bulti* (*Chromis niloticus*), the most delicate of the Nile fish.

The example is taken from a group of three fish of different kinds, used as word-symbol for *rm·w*, "fish," in which it takes the place of honour; but this position is not invariable. The *bulti* is named , *yn·t* (*àn·t*), and is phon. for *yn* (*àn*).

Fig. 45. A centipede (*Myriapod*).

Word-sign for *sp*ʾ (*sepa*) and *sp*. In *Pap. Eb.*, xli., 11, is a verb , which one may guess to mean "to be flexible," "to be jointed," and *l.c.*, lxxviii., 9, is a worm, , apparently living in human flesh. Possibly the centipede shared its name with any worm or grub. In *Pyr. W.*, l. 329, &c., *sp*ʾ is the dead body, perhaps in connexion with the articulated skeleton, or perhaps with the idea of the chrysalis. Cf. *z·t* for the body, *ḫ*ʾ*·t* (*cha·t*) for the corpse. The root must not be confused with that of , *śp·t*, "nome."

Fig. 72; *B. H.*, iii., fig. 33. A bivalve shell of variable form; in O.K. generally a *Unio*, a fine example being in Mar., *M. D.*, Pl. 94. In *Pyr. N.*, l. 1136, it has scalloped edges, and is presumably a sea-shell. Professor Maspero has noticed the resemblance of the sign to the fans used for fanning flame (*Rev. Arch.*, xxxii., p. 27); but though the form in *B. H.*, iii. may suggest this identity, the colour does not, nor do I know of any instance of the sign in which it is furnished with a handle such as is invariably found with the fan.

The name of the shell is not known. Pearl shells engraved with the names of kings are found dating from the XIIth Dynasty, and were evidently valued. *Unios*, &c., are common among prehistoric remains. In the title , we may perhaps read "superintendent of horns, hoofs, feathers, and *shells*," and in some names of metals one sees a similar sign. But here, as so often, we are in want of facsimiles to settle the identity.

The sign is regularly found at all periods in the word *ḫaw·t* (*khaw·t*), "altar," and perhaps only in this word; but it is a peculiarity of the Pyramid Texts that is in them used very commonly, not only as a word-sign, but also as phon. equivalent to for *ḫ*ʾ (*kha*), and apparently for *ḫ* alone in many words. It is not so found again till a very late period. From its special use in spelling the word for "altar," it would seem that the shell was called *ḥ'w·t* rather than *ḥ'*; on the other hand, the name of the lotus leaf, *ḥ'*, is probably derived from the same root, on account of its shell-like outline—or *vice versâ*.

G. Trees, Herbs, Grasses, &c.

Fig. 170. Trunk or branch of tree cut down and roughly trimmed.

Word-sign for , *ẖt* (*khet*) (with radical), "wood," "timber," "tree." Used by phon. tr. for many other words, including the pseudo-derivative (?) *nẖt*, "strong," "strength." Det. of wood and of objects made of wood.

Fig. 57. Pod of carob bean (?).

In *Sign Pap.*, p. xvii., no. 2, this is described as "pod of the *nzm* tree." As *nzm* means "sweet," "pleasant" of flavour, odour, &c., and is the word-sign value of this pod, the latter must be the pod of the carob bean, as has been shown by Loret, *Rec. de Trav.*, xv., 114. The sign is used also in spelling the pseudo(?)-derivative *s̀·nzm*, "sit on a chair."

Fig. 69. Graphic compound of with the phon. . The former seems to represent the first sprout from a root or seed with a bud at the side.

The first element symbolizes (1) yearly growth, and so years and renewal; (2) seasons, since the growth of vegetables took place after the inundation, and at other regular seasons by help of irrigation. Its values are, therefore, (*a*) word-sign, *rnp*, "grow freshly, vigorously," generally written in early texts. *rnp·t* probably means "young vegetables" as an offering. This value may be derived from (*b*) word-sign *rnp·t*, "year," Copt. ⲣⲟⲙⲡⲉ, , in dates , more rarely , (L., *D.*, ii., 116*a*; *Pyr. N.*, l. 754). Not uncommonly a special form, , is found, e.g. *B. H.*, i., Pl. viii., and in many symbolical representations, apparently indicating the succession of years by an artificial multiplication of the buds upon the shoot. Whether (*a*) or (*b*) were derived one from the other is difficult to say. (*c*) It is also word-sign for *rr*, written in *Pyr.* (*T.*, l. 63; *P.*, l. 162), probably meaning "to renew"; and (*d*) word-sign or det. for *tr*, "season of year," "time of day," written ; also phon. for the same value, then written (once perhaps , *N.*, l. 975). (*e*) After O.K. it began to be written after any word ending in . This value is apparently derived from (*c*), the ancient , which now sounded *ry* (*râ*): ancient was thenceforth written , to correspond.

In N.K. there was great confusion in the use of , , .

[*B. H.*, iii., fig. 19.] Herb. The form is very variable in early times. Of the present example M. Loret remarks, "il fait penser à une fleur née à mi-hauteur de la tige, comme par exemple l'*acorus*." In *Medum*, Pl. xv., we have a single stalk terminating in four short shoots irregularly spreading from the top.

Name, *ḥn*, a marsh-plant, referred to as a type of greenness in *Pyr. T.*, l. 100; cf. *El B.*, ii., p. 23, *Pap. Eb.*, and *T. el Y.*, Pl. xxv., ll. 16, 25. Phon. for *ḥn*. Another name for the same (?) marsh-plant is , *ys* (*ȧs*) (Br., *Wtb. Suppl.*, p. 14; *Pap. Eb.*; Maspero, *Ét. Ég.*, i., p. 237); for this value is used with phon. trans., and stands alone by ab. for *ys*, "old" (*Kah. Pap.*, Pl. xx., 24).

Det. of herbaceous plants, and of leaves and twigs of trees.

[*B. H.*, iii., fig. 83.] Flower (?).

The geographical name, , *B. H.*, i., p. 85, has the variant in *B. H.*, i., Pl. vii.

(with the god Chnem). In XXIst Dyn. (MASP., *Momies Royales*, pp. 713-4) occurs (with the god Amen). This sign is therefore the frequent word-sign for *rd* "flourish." It is also word-sign for *mʿr* (*mȧr*), "successful"; later, *mʿrd* (without , SH., *Eg. Insc.*, ii., Pl. 83, l. 11). Probably also it is , the word-sign for *bn*[*r*], "sweet."

Fig. 108. Three curiously-shaped bands, apparently garlands, strings or chains of white flowers, tied together at the top. Such garlands are frequently represented as offerings, &c., on the monuments of the N.K., and remains of such have been found on the N.K. mummies of Deir el Bahri, &c.

Word-sign and phon. for *ms*, meaning "produce" children, "form" images, &c. Probably these elaborate garlands made of white flowers, or woven of separate petals, were named *ms*, "the artificial" as opposed to the simple flowers. At Medinet Habu, in the time of Rameses II. and Rameses III. (DÜM., *Opfer-festliste*, *passim*), they are named , for which *Pap. Har.*, i., 73, l. 5, has a variant , *msb*. This is evidently connected with the word *sb*, "bring," "offer." Is it possible that *msb* is a late word, due to a false etymology deforming an original name *ms*, "artificial garland"?

For construction of garlands see SCHWEINFURTH, *Ueber Pflanzenreste*, *Deutsch. Bot. Ges. Berichte*, 1884, p. 353.

Fig. 106. Reed-head with flower (*Calamus*). The present example is a poor one; detail is shown in *Medum*, Pl. xi., &c.; *B. H.*, i., Pl. xxviii.; see also CH., *Mon.*, ccxxi., 79, for representation of reeds flowering. Cf. for *šḫt* (*sekhet*), "meadow," and *šm*, "herbage," where probably stands for grass heads.

The reed-stem, or its head, is named the *y* (*ȧ*) of the reed (*Pap. Eb.*, xlix., 2; LORET, *Rec. de Tr.*, xiii., 199). Transferred as a word-sign it is often written *y* (*ȧ*) in *Pyr.*, and the plural *yw* (*ȧu*) is transferred to spelling the auxiliary verb *yw* (*ȧu*), "to be" (SETHE, *Ä. Z.*, 1897, p. 6). Alph. for *y* (*ȧ*). *Kah. Pap.*, xix., ll. 59, &c., suggest that the root of the name of is really *y*ʾ, and for this value may sometimes be phon.; but the indications are doubtful. Cf. below, *s.v.* ⊿. Initial seems generally to have been reduced to the sound of ʾ (*alif*), and though is never substituted for it in good writing, in early texts is constantly omitted altogether, even in cases where *y* reappears in the Coptic. In such instances perhaps it had been preserved in some popular dialects, while in the official language it was reduced to *alif*.

After O.K. appears to have been used for *y* at the end of words, but in O.K. it occasionally appears (e.g. in) to mark the dual, where probably is dual (*ywi* = ʾ*wi*), and so stood for the dual ending *wi*.

Figs. 32, 87. Corn on the threshing-floor. With fig. 32 compare *Methen*, L., *D.*, ii., 5, top. The simple form is commoner. It appears to represent a circular heap of corn, or a circular floor covered with grain and surrounded by a wall of bricks or of sheaves. It may be doubted whether the animals were driven round the outside of the stack; the scenes (e.g. *Paheri*, Pl. iii.) and the sign rather indicate that the animals trampled a central space surrounded by heaps of corn in the ear (*v.* Addenda).

Word-sign for *spʾt*, which often means "what is spared" from destruction, "what remains" of an infusion after boiling down the liquid. This sense can easily be connected with the grain that remains on the floor when straw and chaff have been eliminated. But though this is probably the radical sense of the word, in scenes of farm-life it occurs rather with the meaning of the corn that is to be threshed. In tombs of the Vth and VIth Dynasties we see sheaves of corn with short stalks, brought from the field on asses and thrown into heaps, with the inscription , or , which must mean something like "preparing the threshing," "heaping the corn," or "preparing the threshing-floor." In *El B.*, i., Pl. xxxi., where a troop of asses are treading out the corn on a raised heap, the inscription (on fragment 12, which fits to 2) is "threshing the *sp·t* by ...."

Used by rad. ext. and phon. trans. as *sp*.

[*B. H.*, i., Pl. xxviii.] Pool with lotus flowers. The pool may be either oval or rectangular; there may be buds alternating with the flowers, and the flowers may almost rest on the water, or may have long stems (*Medum*, Pl. xix.); but in good instances the flowers always have serrated edges, indicating the petals of lotus. This raises the question whether the *Nelumbium*, or Indian lotus, which rises out of the water, is not sometimes represented; but its absence from Egyptian water-scenes appears to prohibit this explanation. In *Pyr. P.*, l. 440, the flowers on the are termed *nḥb·wt*, with det. a lotus-flower, . The word-sign found in *Pyr.* for "verdant," probably represents papyrus, not lotus, and is therefore distinct from this.

Name, *š'* (*sha*), cf. *Pyr. P.*, l. 440, with *M.*, l. 656, "lotus pools." As these were most important items in gardens, the name became almost synonymous with "garden," "vineyard," &c. Phon. for *š'*.

Fig. 54; *B. H.*, iii., fig. 58. A flower-stem, bent back on itself twice. The object depicted varies, but the general form of the sign is always the same—a stem or band bearing some kind of head, and invariably bent in much the same way. In *Pyr.* sometimes it has the form of a lotus bud, with stem bent in a zigzag, . In the present instance it seems to be a papyrus stem.

Word-sign for *wdn* (*uden*), "heavy." Probably (as opposed to , , , , , , *dbn*, *pḫr* (*pekher*), *wdb* (*udeb*), *qb*, with the general sense of "curve," &c.), signifies crushed or bent down by its own weight. Also in the sense of "offering," *wdn* seems to have the radical meaning of "pile up" offerings, "present in abundance" (cf. , p. 32, for the same idea). (pestle and mortar), distinctly a sign of crushing and weight, frequently replaces in all its meanings.

Fig. 143; *B. H.*, iii., fig. 16. Clump of three papyrus stems.

Word-sign for *ḥ'* (*ha*)—see *B. H.*, iii., p. 9, for a possible explanation—and phon. for the same.

It is sometimes substituted for as word-sign for *mḥ*, "north" (*B. H.*, iii., *l.c.*), for *ydḥ* (*àdh*), "papyrus marsh," and for *y'ḫ* (*àakh*), "be verdant." (The name of the papyrus is *mnḥ*.)

Fig. 125. Papyrus stem, highly conventionalized as usual, the umbel represented as compact (see *B. H.*, iii., pp. 9 *et seqq.*; BORCHARDT, *Pflanzensaüle*, pp. 25 *et seqq.*); scales at the base.

Word-sign for *w'z* (*uaz*), "green," "flourishing." *W'z·t*, "the green," is the name of the goddess of the North (Uazet, Buto), of whom the was probably the symbol. As an amulet or symbol it is named *w'z*, and it is commonly placed in the hand of goddesses—especially in Ptolemaic times—probably as emblem of freshness. The N.K. combination often stands for "the two lands (South and North)," or as adj. for *rs·i*, *mḥ·ti*, "south," "north."

Fig. 66; *B. H.*, iii., fig. 17. Highly conventionalized rush (?).

In *Pyr. M.*, l. 239 = *N.*, l. 616, it is stated

that a large sack or basket, with handle for "transport," *q'r* (*qar*), is made of *twn* (*tun*), "the springy" (cf. Lat. *salix* "osier"!), and the "containing" *neb*-basket (*q.v.*) of *nn·t*, "the limp," i.e. almost certainly the non-resilient rush, from "be weary, motionless." From this name comes the word-sign value *nn*; to avoid its reduction to *n*, and to distinguish it from the next value, *nḫb*, it is in this case always written. It is used to spell the pseudo(?)-causative *śnn*, "image," &c.

The ancient name of El Kab is *Nḫb* (*Nekheb*), usually spelt with this sign, ⊗. Perhaps the rush (*Juncus maritimus*?) was found in the desert valleys behind El Kab, and so symbolized the city. After O.K. the group was reinforced by the vase Ō, thus ⊗, Ō ⊗, possibly referring to some other product of the place (natron?). This group is always written with the ∫, and is only found in the name of the city and the derived name of its presiding goddess, the vulture Nekhebt (*v. Pyr. M.*, l. 762, for the spelling), except that in very late times the tall rose-lotus *Nelumbium* (?) was called by confusion, on account of its name *nḫb*.

As the vulture-goddess Nekhebt was representative of the South, the resemblance of to and is very remarkable; compare the quotation from Plutarch by Loret (in the next column), which may perhaps refer in particular to the present sign.

Fig. 109. The plant-symbol of rule in Upper Egypt.

The symbol is named, *Kah. Pap.*, Pl. iii., l. 2: perhaps *św·t*; cf. also a similar word in *l.c.*, Pl. xxxiv., l. 19, and "serfs (?)," *Methen*, L., *D.*, ii., 3, 6, probably to be read *św·tiw* (*śu·tiu*), and , in *Pap. Eb.* = in the corrupt writing of *Anastasi IV.* (viii., l. 12). If this reads *św·t św·ti*, it would perhaps mean "feather," i.e. "plume-head, of the (?)"; otherwise it would mean "king's plumes," as a plant-name. The plant occurs in *Todt.*, xcix., *Einl.*, see the M.K. texts, MASPERO, *Trois Années*, p. 163, &c. If any of these words read *św·t*, they may be the origin of the phon. value *św* of, in good writing always distinguished as.

The King of Upper Egypt is designated, generally abbreviated to *stn* or *stni*. is also transferred to the homophonous *stni*, "butcher." *stn*, as the name of the crown of Upper Egypt, has as yet been found only in late texts, but might be the origin of the *nisbe* or adjectival form *stni*, unless the above is to be read *stn*, and is thus its early equivalent. If this be the case, we have to seek elsewhere for the origin of = *św*. A conspicuous example of this value is in the word *św*, "he," absolute pronoun of third pers. masc. sing.; possibly the king was taken as the "He" *par excellence*. Cf., perhaps symbol of "father," representing the suffix "he," "his."

[*B. H.*, iii., fig. 20.] Sedge (*Scirpus*). Loret remarks: "L'identification du approche peu à peu de la vérité. C'est bien, en effet, une graminée à epillets roux. Au lieu de *scirpus*, j'y verrais un *juncus*, parceque Plutarque nous enseigne que, pour designer le *sud* et le *Roi*, les Égyptiens dessinent un jonc (θρύον). Pourtant il a pu confondre un jonc et un *scirpus*." The reference to Plutarch is to *De Iside et Osiride*, cap. 36. Since the publication of *B. H.*, iii., Borchardt has supplied some interesting remarks on the plant of Upper Egypt in his excellent work *Die Aegyptischen Pflanzensaüle*, p. 20.

Word-sign for *qmʿ* (*qemâ*), "south country," "south," with phon. transf., frequently written; and for, adj. "southern," frequently written , also , i.e. with , which may be the same plant before flowering.

H. Sky, Earth, and Water.

⊙ Fig. 10. The sun's disk, coloured red and edged with yellow.

Word-sign (1) for *Rʿ* (*Rā*), the name of the Sun-god—in *Pyr.* usually written ⊙ alone—and no doubt of the sun itself. = *rʿ nb* (*rā neb*) is a common phrase for "every day," lit. "each sun." (2) For *hrw* (*hru*), "day," as opposed to night and also as a measure of time. (3) In dates, days of the month are denoted by ⊙, in the XIIth Dynasty often written ⊙, with the geographical det. , as indicating limited time. In Coptic the corresponding word is ⲥⲟⲩ, a word often found in late Egyptian texts as , *ssw* (*sesu*), for the day of the month. This word existed at a fairly early period (, plu. in *Paheri*, Pl. ix., l. 4, meaning "dates for festivals"), and Erman has suggested recently that it is the true reading for ⊙ as "day of the month."

Det. of words concerning the sun and times and seasons, the sun being the principal regulator of days, seasons, and years.

Figs. 37, 137. A semicircular figure formed of half a disk and four concentric bands of different colours—blue, green, and red. A fifth and cresting band, sometimes marked with radiating lines, does not extend to the diameter. Cf. the jewelled hieroglyph in *Dahchour*, Pls. xv., 1; xix., i.

The meanings of the word-sign , *ḫʿ* (*khā*)—*not* (cf. Χεφρην for and Coptic ϣⲁⲓ)—are "royal crown," "to be crowned," "to appear in glory" (like the sun-god), used of king or god coming forth from palace or temple. Also we have (*Pyr. T.*, l. 36; *P.*, l. 387), *ḫʿ n tꜣ* (*khā n ta*), the "*khā* of earth," i.e. the place on earth in which Ra (and the dead king likewise) purifies himself, apparently before he rises into heaven, in the morning (?). In the same way a temple is called the , *ḫʿy* (*khāy*) of a god, i.e. his resting-place on earth, to which he descends and whence he also ascends. thus seems to represent pictorially the effulgence of the sun at the point where he rests on earth. (Though the "*khā* of earth" as a place for the sun-god's purification by ablution may suggest it, nothing else bears out the idea that may be intended for a rainbow.) The other senses of this word are easily obtained from the notion of divine effulgence.

Also phon. for *ḫʿ* (*khā*), but probably not before the XIXth Dynasty.

★ Fig. 31. Star of five points, the present example having a disk at the centre; the rays here look broad and solid, and are marked with transverse lines at intervals, like the fire-stick, fig. 42.

(1) The name is ★ *šb*, "star," lit. "instructor," "guiding star" (cf. *Siut*, Tomb i., l. 264, "I was (a man), the guiding star (★) of his equals, the director of those older than he"). Hence, being from the root *šbꜣ* (*sba*), it was transferred to various words as *šbꜣ*. (2) Another word-sign value is *dwꜣ* (*dua*), "early morning" and "praise," apparently because to the Egyptians, who retired into their houses soon after sunset and rose before dawn, stars and starlight were much connected with early morning, which was therefore written ★⊙. To *dwꜣ* the word for 5 is closely similar, and the representation of the star with five points is clearly connected with this circumstance. (3) The hours of the night being regulated by the stars, "hour," *wnwt* (*unut*), is written .

★ is also det. of stars and of hours.

[*B. H.*, i., Pl. xxviii.; cf. *B. H.*, iii.,

fig. 80.] Hilly desert, coloured to represent sand and rocks or stones.

Word-sign for 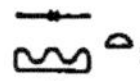, L., *D.*, ii., 3, "desert," "foreign land," and perhaps "foreign tribe"; usually spelt 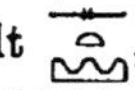, but rarely 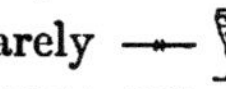 *sm·t* (L., *D.*, ii., 112*d*; *Ä. Z.*, 1874, 35). According to Erman (*Ä. Z.*, 1892, 10) *sm·t* is the true reading.  in the neighbourhood of *s* or *š* seems curiously negligeable; cf. *šmkt·t* spelt with  *šk*. For the title *mr sm·wt* compare L., *D.*, ii., 100*b*; *B. H.*, ii., Pl. xxiv., with *B. H.*, i., tomb iii., *passim* (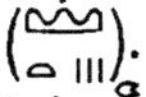).

Another word for desert is  *h'šh·t* (*khaškhet*), Mar., *Mast.*, 188, which may be quite distinct from  *h's·t* (*khas·t*) in *Pyr.* (with). It is possible that one or other of these words is an occasional reading for , and we have as yet no certain reading for the sign as word-sign for "foreign tribe" (*P. S. B. A.*, 1897, 297).

Det. of desert, foreign lands, &c. (as opposed to the alluvial land of Egypt).

 Fig. 38. A desert mountain, showing a valley between two crests (pinkish yellow variegated with red for the stones; at the base a line of green to indicate fertile land). Cf. *Medum*, Pls. xiv., xxviii., and p. 30. As  (fertile ground) means a "slope," "height," so , a desert mountain, was chosen to represent hill or rock, while 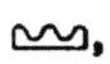, a kind of plural form, stands for "desert"; but in the earliest instances (*Medum*, *l.c.*)  is more like two hills and less like two .

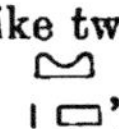,  *zw* (*zu*), is "mountain," "hill," "rock," lit. "the evil," "worthless" (see below, *ad fin.*). Sometimes, however, it seems to read 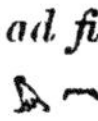 *mn*, "rock," lit. "the firm (?)"; e.g. the common title of Anubis, 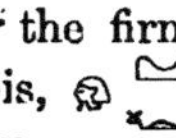 "upon his (?) hill," or "upon the hill of the  (*q.v.*)" is rendered by 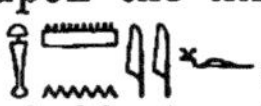, , *tp mny f*, in the remarkable inscription of Auabra (*Dahchour*, p. 104). Traces of this value are seen also in late writing.

, *dw*, "evil," is read by some  *hw* (*khu*), apparently on the ground of its varying in very late times with , a word of similar significance. , however, in late texts is often confused with , so that confusion with  is not surprising. The two words occur separately in the Prisse Papyrus, and cannot be identical.  "worthless," "evil," is, in fact, of allied meaning to  "desert," "mountain," which had always an evil significance to the agricultural mind of the Egyptians. In the Kahun calendar (*Kah. Pap.*, Pl. xxv.), and elsewhere, red ink was employed in writing the word  "evil (day)." Red, the colour of sand, as opposed to black, the colour of alluvium, was considered ominous, evidently on account of its connexion with the sterile desert, , , the haunt of demons.

 Fig. 50. A narrow oval ridge or expanse of sandy desert, coloured as . We may probably consider this sign as representing (1) a sandy island in the river; (2) an island of sand appearing through the alluvium, such as the Arabs still call *gezireh*; (3) any sandy ridge or expanse.

As word-sign we have it in  "island," which varies in late times with ,  *y't* (*àa·t*), and so perhaps reads *y'* (*àa*); this is a common word in Egyptian geography for islands both in sea and river, and so probably denotes also sand-islands in the alluvium.

Det. or id. of [illegible] = [illegible], [illegible] *y'h·t* (*àakh·t*), "horizon"; the dual or adjectival form [illegible] is commonly written [illegible] by abbreviation, [illegible] "the two horizons," each horizon being sandy desert according to Egyptian ideas. In O.K. the sign is a common det. of names of districts and places, probably on account of their being in sandy districts or connected with a Deltaic gezîreh. Early towns in the Delta were founded on such "islands." Later, it became det. of certain specific localities only, as in the present case, where it is used with *Ta-zeser*, the sandy domain of Anubis, god of the dead.

In N.K. , is phon. at the beginning of words, apparently for 𓇋𓄿 *y*ʾ (*ȧa*).

Cf. **Fig. 14.** Apparently compound id. of the sand-island and the water-line 𓈖. It seems not to occur before N.K.

Word-sign for 𓇋 *Ymn* (*Ȧmen*), the name of the god Amen in late times. Perhaps indicates *mn*, "firm," by combining *m*(?)·*t*, Coptic ⲙⲟⲩⲓ (fem.), "island," and *n*. In very late times it is used for 𓐍 *Nẖn*.

𓈇 [*B. H.*, iii., fig. 95.] Flat alluvial land, coloured black (L., *D.*, ii., 20), later blue. Often , with three grains o (*q.v.* p. 34), indicating the sand underlying the alluvium. These grains are wrongly called "3 pits (or caves)" in the *Sign Pap.*, p. xiv., l. 4.

Word-sign for 𓏏𓄿 *t*ʾ (*ta*), "earth," "black soil" (e.g. under the nails), "alluvial land." In late times phon. for *t*ʾ (*ta*).

By id. trans., det. of 𓆓·𓏏 *z·t*, "eternity," as being of unbounded horizon (*B. H.*, iii., p. 30). Cf. 𓈖.

𓈎 **Fig. 71.** Mound of earth (not desert), natural or artificial; coloured black, like 𓈇, in O.K. (L., *D.*, ii., 21), later green or grey. Desert slopes are represented with similar outline but different colour, as fig. 60.

In *B. H.*, iii., p. 5, this sign is derived from the word 𓈎𓄿 "high ground"; but in *Pyr. M.*, l. 202, there is a word 𓈎𓄿𓄿𓈎 *q*ʾʾ (*qaa*), determined by a sign like 𓈎, and in L., *D.*, iii., 24, *d* (W), it is given as 𓈎𓄿𓇋𓇋 *q*ʾ*y* (*qay*), meaning "lofty place," "pile," "eminence." The weak radical 𓄿 is neglected in the alphabetic value *q* of 𓈎, but 𓈎 seems to have served also as phon. for 𓈎𓄿 (as and similarly served for 𓏏𓄿 and 𓊪𓄿, and for the same reasons), and required no other biliteral with 𓄿, though combinations with 𓄿 are very numerous. On the other hand, the alphabetic characters , 𓈖, and show no trace of such a use, their derivation implying no 𓄿; the combination of these with 𓄿 was so rare that no phon. was needed for it.

𓈎𓈎 (Cf. fig. 71.) Two heaps of provisions. This group is treated here because in the Tomb of Paheri, according to a copy by Miss Pirie, the two 𓈎 in are of the same form and colour as fig. 71 taken from the same line of inscription (*Paheri*, Pl. iii., cornice-line). In L., *D.*, ii., 103*a*, we see a heap of corn of precisely the form of 𓈎.

In *Pyr.* "eat," varies with , , (?) *wnm* (*unem*); and is used as phonetically equivalent to *wnm* (*unem*), another form of the loan-word (?), ימין, *ymn* (*ȧmen*), "right hand," "West" (Erman, *Ä. Z.*, 1893, pp. 82, 127; 1894, 67). For the later history of this word see , p. 37. Besides the word-sign value, 𓈎𓈎 is also in *Pyr.* det. of , *wšb* (*us̱heb*), *šb*, "provisions," and of *bʿḥ* (*bȧḥ*), "abundance." It is therefore id. of eatables, abundance of provisions; but to make its meaning clearer it is usually, in *Pyr.*, accompanied by auxiliary dets., or , in a manner very unusual with other signs. The doubling of the heap is not merely intensive. In *Ptahhetep*, Pl. xli., table of offerings, 4th row, 3rd col. from right, we have 𓈎𓈎 *gświ šbw*(?), "two halves, or sides, of provisions," which may be explained by *B. H.*, i., Pl. xvii., table of offerings, 2nd row, 9th col. from left, *p*ʾ·*t n·t wdn wp m gś·wi*, "food of heaped-offering divided into two sides (or halves)." A mass of offerings—common breadstuff?—was thus perhaps made into two heaps on either hand of the recipient, and provisions were probably served in the same way at any plentiful feast in the earlier times, when abundance of food was doubtless much considered. In L., D., ii., 70, *gś* is determined by *three* heaps, ▵▵▵ (for the plural), the colour of which is black, like that of the bread and of ▵ = *q* (*l.c.*, ii., 69).

▦ Cf. Fig. 175 and *B. H.*, iii., Frontispiece. Land-area marked with rectangular lines for irrigation canals (?) at regular intervals, the ends open or closed by lines, ▨. In *El B.*, i., Pl. xxvii. 11, a plain rectangle ▭, perhaps an unfinished ▨, seems to take the place of the latter. In *Siut*, Tomb i., l. 228, the downward lines are oblique.

Word-sign for ▯o𝕤•◦ *śp'·t*, "nome," "territory of a city," and for ⅂𝕤◦•◦ *z'·t·t* (*zat·t*) (meaning ?). (See *Kah. Pap.*, p. 31.) Det. of nomes and of ▵𝕤→ "south country."

〰 Figs. 12, 176. Waved line of the surface of water, coloured black or grey. Cf. *Medum, passim.*

The waved line is constantly seen in representations of pools of water, &c., and seems properly to belong to the rippled surface, but it became the sign of water in general. Thus, while the curved stream of water pouring downward from the hand or from a vessel is often smooth in early times, or only slightly waved—to show spiral flow—yet even in the tomb of *Methen* (L., D., ii., 4) there is an example of its being waved like 〰 as a conventional representation of water.

The single 〰 has not yet been found as a distinct word sign. It is used almost exclusively as alph. for *n*, and *n* is an important element in the words for water. Thus 〰/ooo 𝕤 *Nw* (*Nu*) is "the primordial water," 〰/↺ 𝕤 *nw* is a "stream of water." In *Pyr. N.*, l. 132, 〰 seems actually to be det. of the latter.

As det., 〰 occurs apparently in the sense of "level" in the word ⌐⌐ "eternity," written also ⌐⌐. Sometimes this latter may be read *n z'·t*, but in many cases (*Pyr.*, e.g. *W.*, 521, &c., &c., and in *Ptahhetep*, Pl. xxxix., ▱▮〰⌐⌐) it can only be explained as det. of level surface, such as water always presents, like —, ◦𝕤 *t'* (*ta*), "level land" (see *B. H.*, iii., p. 30). The instances of this use are too numerous to be accounted for as due to the confusion of 〰 and — in hieratic.

〰〰, i.e. three 〰, is the plural word 𝕤𝕓 *mw* (*mn*), "water," later used as singular (ERM., *Pluralbildung*, p. 14, *Gram.*, § 45). In a few (pseudo-compound) words the sign 〰〰 is phon. for *mw*. 〰〰—which certainly better than 〰 represents a rippled surface—is also the regular det. of water and of liquids.

▥ Fig. 90. A rectangular tank or artificial pool (cf. *Medum, passim*); in N.K. often represented as empty, ▭, though in O.K. this may have a distinct meaning. The ordinary printed form ▭ is taken from linear hieroglyphic writing, in which the distinction of the tank sign from other rectangular signs has been reduced to two purely conventional strokes.

A tank, pool, or lake is named ▥▽▮, ◦ *ś* (*she*), whence this sign obtains its alphabetic value *ś*. It is also det. of *ḫnt*, "pool," "pleasure garden (surrounding a pond)."

▽ Fig. 58; *B. H.*, iii., fig. 88. This may be taken for a section of a water-channel with running water, or a pond, or a transparent vessel containing liquid, or a crucible containing molten metal, or the matrix in the ground into which the molten metal was run to form ingots. In good texts it is often ▽, i.e. with surface not rippled; ▽ is a form of the base period.

(1) ▽ varies with ▽, ◦▮ *pḥ* (*peḥ*), which means a marsh or pool left by the inundation. But this use is not known before N.K.

(2) In a great number of words it is phon.

for *by*ʾ (*bȧa*). A clue to the reason may perhaps be found in the word , *by*ʾ (*bȧa*), "liquid abyss(?) of heaven," "aethereal space," probably with the idea as it were of a great lake or stream of aether in which the sun and heavenly bodies travel. Or we may prefer the following explanation:—There is a substance called , ; possibly, from the det., it denotes transparent crystal, or perhaps metal. The sun's throne in heaven is said to be *by*ʾ (*bȧa*), "of crystal(?)," or adamant, or "smoothly gliding" (like a sledge). Heaven itself, or space, is "the liquid stream" (*Ptahhetep*, Pl. xxxix.), or "the crystal(?) aether." There is also the verb , , *by*ʾ (*bȧa*), "vanish(?)," or "glide smoothly," like a sledge, or perhaps "melt" like metal. Gliding and transparency, one or both of which ideas are included in the root *by*ʾ, are both qualities of liquid.

(3) By id. trans. stands for the female principle in , (= *vulva*); the reading uncertain, perhaps *k*ʾ·*t* or *ḥm*·*t*, or *yt* (*ȧt*), which occasionally occurs (cf. *Kah. Pap.*, p. 6, and for examples see Loret, *Rec. de Trav.*, xviii., 198). It occurs in the det. of the word in *Pyr.*, and in , *ḥm*·*t*, "woman." Probably it is from the last word that obtains its very common value as phon. for *ḥm*.

Fig. 29. Grain of sand, pebble, or little pellet (here coloured white, and repeated until the number indicates five). In the compound sign for , "earth," the grains, which are three in number to denote the plural, seem to indicate the sand that was known to underlie the alluvium.

At times seems to be word-sign for , *ṯ*ʾ (*ṯha*), "pellet," from *ṯ*ʾ, "take," as we speak of a "pinch" of anything. is det. of sand, pebbles, &c., and of pellets. It is often used instead of to denote the plural, and—especially in *Pyr.*— denotes the singular, in place of (*q.v.*).

I. Buildings and their Parts.

Fig. 142; *B. H.*, iii., fig. 76. Conventional figure apparently representing in a summary manner the plan of a village with cross streets within a circular enclosure.

Word-sign for town or city, . Det. of names of villages, cities, and sometimes more widely of inhabited regions.

The reading is *n*·*t* (Erm., *Pluralbildung*, p. 9), or perhaps better *nn*·*t*. The name of the goddess (*nn*·*t* (?), *v.*), especially as representing the lower hemisphere of heaven, is written , in N.K.; in *Pyr.* it is (*W.*, l. 219), (*W.*, ll. 289, 557), (*M.*, l. 455, cf. *W.*, l. 239).

Cf. **Fig. 34.** Rectangular enclosure wall with battlements, usually represented as very narrow.

Word-sign for *ynb* (*ȧnb*), "fortified enclosure wall," "wall"; cf. Br., *Wtb.*, *Suppl.*, 92, for variant with *ynb*, also *Pyr. N.*, l. 955, for rad. ext.

Det. of "wall," and (in O.K.) of building.

Fig. 30; *B. H.*, iii., fig. 62. Palatial courtyard. There are two main types of this hieroglyph, the first, modelled on the lines of , the second on those of (*qq.v.*), each highly elaborated, as befits the sign of a royal residence.

(1) (Type, fig. 30, &c.). This is represented by the plan of a nearly square enclosure, the wall of which is carried only half way along the front and then turns in at a right angle, enclosing an inner court, the outer court, of the same size, being entirely open in front. The entrance of

the inner court is at the inner end of the dividing wall, and in the front corner farthest from that entrance stands the tower-like palace, (*q.v.*). The enclosure wall and the tower are crested with *cheker* ornament, (PETRIE, *Dec. Art*, p. 101), or with overhanging battlements. The tower is not essential to the figure, and is often absent, ; , in which it occupies the whole front of the inner court, is an exceptional form. or , for the name *wsḫ·t*, is commonly placed in the entrance.

(2) Type is seldom found in the tables of offerings (as an exception see L., *D.*, ii., 67, 6th col. from right), but is very common in O.K. titles (L., *D.*, ii., 63, &c., &c.), though later it does not seem to occur. This shows a complete rectangle, battlemented and containing a *cheker*-topped palace in one corner, as well as to the left. In *Pyr. N.*, l. 764, this sign has a battlemented building in the corner, containing , which is probably symbolic of the deity, though seldom used in O.K. with that signification. On the analogy of the , we may consider that in this type the palace-tower is built over or near to the entrance (compare the position of the tower at Medinet Habu); in also there would probably be a private entrance to the tower through the adjoining wall.

Word-sign for *wsḫ·t* (*usekh·t*), "the broad," "roomy," a name used perhaps not only for the courtyard but also for a wide hall.

In *Pyr.* with its variants (type 1, but without the palace sign, never the complete rectangle, type 2), is det. of *sbḫ* (*sebekh*), which apparently means "surround with protection."

Fig. 146. Plan of a nearly square enclosure resembling the (*q.v.*, type 1), but plain, without battlements, *cheker* ornament, or building shown within.

The word which was the origin of the biliteral phonetic value *ḥ'* (*ha*) and the alph. value *h* (see and for similar usages), is probably connected with the root "enter." , with det. of land-area, more fully written *ḥ'y·t* (*hay·t*), is perhaps the name of the outer or entrance court indicated by the sign, and so the origin of its phonetic values.

[Cf. *B. H.*, iii., fig. 5.] Plan of rectangular enclosure, without battlements, but with small building in the corner. It seems to be a less grandiose form of (*v.* , type 2). The inner building, which is square in the early O.K., is best explained as a tower to defend the entrance; cf. Maspero's valuable note (*P.S.B.A.*, xii., 247). In good periods the narrow type is invariable, except in the numerous cases when names and words are written inside the sign; it may then be enlarged horizontally into a square or even an oblong, and the inner building placed in a top corner, or sometimes omitted altogether, according as space is required for the sign or signs to be inserted.

Word-sign for *ḥ·t*, "fenced city," "(fortified) Residence" of king, governor, or god. *ḥ·t-ntr* is a "temple," in the widest sense, with all its varied inhabitants. In some of the cases in which the name of the Residence is written within , this sign is probably only det. of the kind of place. "governor of a ," seems to be the title of the principal sheikhs or lesser governors having citadel, or official fortified and garrisoned, Residences.

Fig. 193; *B. H.*, iii., fig. 56. Plan of the brick walls of a rectangular chamber, with entrance in the middle of the long side; Borchardt quotes with approval the opinion of Steindorff, that represents simply the wall of a (roofless) courtyard. Either explanation seems to fit the case. The elongated type is a late invention to supply an alternative form in grouping hieroglyphs.

Word-sign for *pr*, "house," with weak final *r*. When used by rad. ext., or phon. trans. for *pr*, complementary is added; and *p*[*r*]*sn*, the name of a kind of cake or loaf, varies from the earliest times with , although in the compound = פרעה, "Pharaoh," the *r* was fully retained.

Det. of buildings of all sorts.

Figs. 89, 119. Palace; apparently a tower of two storeys; the diagonal line in the upper half may mark the position of a staircase to the roof. The tower is crowned with *cheker* ornament, and the lower storey is gaily decorated with bands of colour. Cf. . Borchardt's view, that it is really a piece of fringed mat-work, can hardly be sustained.

Word-sign for *ʿḥʿ* (*àḥà*), "king's palace."

Fig. 15. Façade of a shrine or building made of or imitating wattle-and-daub work, with torus edging, &c. (cf. PETRIE, *Dec. Art*, pp. 97-100), and raised on a platform of earth(?) sloping to either side, as in fig. 8. For a somewhat different form see *Pyr. N.*, l. 989. In *Ptahhetep*, Pl. xxxiii., it appears to take the place of ▽ in the symbol of the god Shesemu.

This is the model for a regular type of tomb-stela (cf. *Ptahhetep*, Pl. xxxix.), and in early examples of these stelae the dedications upon them are in the first place to Anubis, , "chief of the divine hall," or "shrine" (see *Ptahhetep*, pp. 32, 33). Within the were supposed to take place the meals of the deceased, and probably within it he rested as in his own private apartments. The reading of the name of the structure, which is generally connected with Anubis, is still unknown. In *Pyr.* it is called (*W.*, ll. 15, 258); unfortunately the reading of is here uncertain; perhaps it indicates basket-work, wattle-work, like the later . In L., *D.*, ii., 112*d*, there is a variant , which may indicate *ys-ntr* (*às-neter*), "divine chamber," or *sḥ ntr*, "divine hall," as the reading of .

Fig. 103. Open hut or shelter made of a framework of reeds bound together, the roof slightly arched and supported by a central forked pole, . In *Medum*, Pl. xiii., the pole is (*q.v.* fig. 116).

Word-sign for *sḥ*, "summer house," "booth," "tent," "canopy," a name most frequently applied to a light wooden construction of the form of one of the canopies in , open in front and at the sides, as an airy but effective shelter from the sun. Under this a grandee could sit in the open air when presiding at an inspection (*El B.*, i., Pl. xix.), or, with his wife at his side, enjoy the busy scenes of outdoor life (*Paheri*, Pl. iv.). In *Ptahhetep*, Pl. xxxix., there is a shelter of this kind over a portable chair: this testifies to its extreme lightness. Used also with phon. trans. as *sḥ*.

Word-sign also for *ḥb*, "festival." Used in this value too with phon. trans., but after O.K. invariably accompanied by, and generally compounded with, the det. (see the next sign). This use indicates that the shelter, like our tents, might be of large size to hold a considerable number of people. Cf., perhaps, the "feast of tabernacles," Lev. xxiii.

In late times it is confused with a rather similar sign reading *ʿrq* (*àrq*).

Figs. 9, 178. Graphic compound of the *seh*, , with id. of a festival, (*q.v.*). This compound is usual in N.K. as word-sign for *ḥb*, "festival." Used with phon. trans.

Fig. 8. On a raised platform, coloured green (earth?, cf. fig. 15, &c.), two portable (?) thrones, (cf. fig. 65), are placed back to back under a double canopy with curved roof.

The reading of the sign is *šd*, or rather perhaps *ḥb šd*, usually written or , but also alone. Word-sign for the jubilee festival of the king, held properly at the end of thirty years—a month of years—

apparently reckoned from his proclamation as crown prince or king (SETHE, *Ä. Z.*, 1898, 64). At the celebration of the jubilee the king sat first as King of Upper Egypt on one of the thrones, and then as King of Lower Egypt on the other; see the figures in L., *D.*, ii., 115*a*; L., *D.*, iii., 74*d*; NAVILLE, *Bubastis*, p. 3 *et seqq.*

Fig. 191. Perhaps a squared block of building stone. (The exact provenance of this sign is uncertain, and it is difficult to identify.)

Word-sign for *ynr* (*åner*), "stone," and det. of names, &c., of stone.

Figs. 78, 169. Two pieces of wood crossed at right angles and joined. In the O.K. with equal arms, (*Methen*, *Ptahhetep*).

Word-sign for the adj. , *ymi* (*åmi*), fem. *ym·t*, plu. *ym·w*, "that which is in," derived from the preposition *m*, "in." The meaning suggests that the sign represents a piece of joiner's work, the two bars being carefully fitted together with a rebate, so being "that which is fitted or fixed in."

But as was pointed out by ERMAN (*Ä. Z.*, 1893, p. 127, cf. 1894, p. 67), by a curious accident it was applied also to quite a different root, as follows:—

In M.K. the verb *wnm*, "eat" (see), appears in two fixed spellings, and . In cursive writing is identical with , and in and after the Hyksos period (*Math. Pap.*, Pl. xxiii., but not *Bul. Pap.*, ii., 45, of the XIIIth Dyn.) an is regularly added to the second group in hieratic; thenceforward in the N.K. the word "eat" appears in hieroglyphics as . The corresponding Coptic word is ⲟⲩⲱⲙ (*wôm*), and it seems altogether that the *n* of *wnm*, "eat," was lost early, so that the word became *wm*, just as , which is *hnmm·t* in *Pyr.*, became *hmm·t* in N.K. To spell the word , as in O.K., was now no longer appropriate. The first change was to , and then began to be written in hieratic, and easily became in transcribing into hieroglyphs. The group thus became the word-group for all the derivatives of , *wm* (*um*), viz. "the eating ulcer," "the devouring flame," &c. (*v.* Addenda).

It is remarkable that in N.K. , originally only another spelling of *wnm* (see above), is retained in religious inscriptions by the side of , as if a different word (*Paheri*, Pls. iii., iv., cornice line); probably it is to be pronounced *wnm*, while the more popular word is *wm*.

In very late texts, in the group , *wndw* (*undu*), "cattle," &c., replaces , owing to its form in cursive writing.

The original value, *ymi* (*åmi*), is often distinguished by prefixed , thus: .

Figs. 88 105; *B. H.*, iii., fig. 41. Wooden clamp. In O.K. it is a straight piece of wood.

The uses of the I are difficult to define. For the early period we may perhaps give the following statement of its uses:—

(1) As a numeral = *wꜥ* (*uå*), "one"; often written .

(2) As det. of unity. From this it has the following derived uses:

a. In *Pyr.*, to indicate a concrete meaning, it is placed after the whole word, generally after a word-sign or det., e.g. *hft* (*kheft*), "enemy"; *st*, "duck"; *ng*, "bull" (both last, *Pyr. P.*, l. 441. ∘ is sometimes substituted for ı in *Pyr.*) And in like manner, ı is often placed after a single sign when it expresses the whole of a name, either with or without the fem. ending.

b. When a sign is used as transferred word-sign with the full phonetic value of the name, the is often transferred with it, e.g. , , , , are all found for *z·t*, "body," or for *š'* (*ša*) for "back," and or *y* (*á*) for "O!" After O.K. the use of in such cases becomes the rule (Erm., *Gram.*, § 51).

In M. and N.K., in such cases as , *t'* (*ta*), "land," and *s*, "person," the det. is added after , for the sake of distinction, as and are in hieratic scarcely distinguishable.

The geographical det. (in M.K. often , from the hieratic?) is usually accompanied in M. and N.K. by the which belongs to it when used as a word-sign.

After O.K. the suffix of 1st pers. sing. is often replaced by .

The numerals up to 9 are expressed by repeated; each of them has its own name (Erman, *Gram.*, § 141). The following are interesting:—

represents the numeral 2, named *šn*, and is from the earliest times det. of duality, especially marking the dual of the masc. nouns ending in *wi*. In this case it is often written in *Pyr.* , e.g. = *ʿwi* (*áwi*), "two hands." It is probable too that can be found with the dual of fem. words ending in *wti* (*uti*), which, however, in ancient times were generally written .

Gradually became employed for the adjectival and other forms of roots in which the termination was the same as that of the dual, *wi*, *wti*; such were now written , ; and then for any terminal *i*, this being the distinctive sound common to the two duals, masc. and fem.

represents the numeral 3, , *ḫmt* (*khemt*), with phon. transf. Also det. of plural, and later of collectives.

, Coptic ϥⲧⲟⲩ (*tiw*); the ancient name not quite certain. See ★, and .

Fig. 116. Wooden column lying on the ground for use as the central pole of a ; see Petrie, *Medum*, Pl. x. and p. 30; *Dec. Art*, p. 76; also Borchardt, *Pflanzensäule*, p. 56 (who seems to have overlooked the very early example at Medum). It is seldom placed upright in good texts, though this is allowed even in O.K. (*Ptahhetep*, xxxviii., left).

Word-sign and phon. for *ʿ'* (*áa*), meaning "lid," "great," "continue in a certain state." It is not clear that it is a name of a column, though there are signs of this (*Kah. Pap.*, xiii., 2, and in late texts). *ʿ'*, "great," may be simply an epithet of the roof-support.

Fig. 139; *B. H.*, iii., fig. 49. Door-bolt: well known from the pictures, and from a wooden shrine in the Cairo Museum, to have been used for fastening folding doors on the outside. On each leaf two bronze rings held a (one bolt being considerably above the other), which was shot into a third ring attached to the other leaf of the door. In the Medum sculptures, "the form of the door-bolt *s* is remarkably contracted in the middle, and has a double line along the neck (*Medum*, Pl. xiii.). Such lines usually show string, as on the tied up necks of bags (Pls. xiii., xv.), and here it seems likely that the middle of the bolt had a string round it which could be sealed on to the door to prevent it being moved" (Petrie, *Medum*, p. 31). The breaking of the seal of a shrine entailed a special ceremony (*Ab.*, i., p. 57). Borchardt, *Ä. Z.*, 1897, p. 105, explains the string as for drawing a bolt from the outside when the door was fastened on the inside (*v.*).

The name of the bolt was "the passer" (*Pyr. N.*, l. 688; cf. *Ab.*, i., pp. 56, 58). This is presumably to be read *s*, though in *Pyr.* it varies with (*T.*, l. 162), which is probably a religious symbol derived from the bolt. The name , cf. *ss* (?) (*Ab.*, i., p. 58), is perhaps a kind of dual, on account of the bolts being two in number; but either name may be the origin of the alphabetic value *s* of —•— (*v.* Addenda).

J. Vases and Pottery: Fire.

[*B. H.*, iii., fig. 35*a.*] Stone jug with long handle from rim to body, and small loop handle opposite to it, upon the body. In the present instance the jug is of alabaster.

General word-sign for *ḫnm* (*chnem*); this may be connected with the word *ḫnm·t*, "well," which might be used as a term for a large jar. But one of the seven sacred oils, named *n·ḫnm*, "of (the god?) Chnem," is usually figured as contained in a jar of this shape. , *B. H.*, iii., fig. 100, represents a jar of this unguent.

Fig. 101. Slender water-bottle, often represented with a stopper. In O.K. the upper part is black instead of blue, a circumstance which Dr. Walker has suggested is to be explained by the black tops of much of the "prehistoric" pottery (see Petrie, *Naqada*, p. 37); red with black or blue rim may therefore be regarded as colouring distinctive of vessels of pottery.

Name, , *ḥs·t*, "the chilly" (?), especially on O.K. coffins (*Miss. Fr.*, i., 200-1, and Pl. ii.); later, cf. Br., *Wtb.* Maspero, *Horhotep* (*Miss. Fr.*, i., p. 136), restores in the label applying to two spouted vases, (shown *l.c.*, Pl. xii.). This is confirmed by the fact that in inferior writing the hieroglyph occasionally has the spout. These *hes* vessels, much used in ceremonial libations, were frequently made in bronze and precious metals, though the picture indicates a pottery original.

Word-sign for *ḥs* in all its meanings.

Fig. 127; *B. H.*, iii., fig. 48. Spouted *hes*-vase, with water pouring from it, and with or without a stand, .

Word-sign for *qbḥ*, "cold water"; used also as det. of and , "be cool," "make cool," but not in *Pyr.*, where (a tree) takes its place in this capacity.

Fig. 6. Group of stoppered *hes*-vases, three or four in number, the ends of a cloth hanging over the shoulders. The number three is the general indication of plurality in this sign, but the definite number of four, , is common from the earliest times, e.g. four occur in *Medum*, Pl. ix. (*Rahotep*), three in Pls. xviii., xxiii. (*Nefermaat*). In L., *D.*, iii., 23, S, by exception the four vessels are without the cloth.

The sign is the ordinary word-symbol for *ḫnt* (*khent*), especially with the meanings "front," "foremost," "forward." The *first* operation in the ceremonial feasts of the "table of offerings," and probably in all such religious ceremonies, was the washing of the table with the four *hes*-vases of water (see e.g. Maspero, *Table d'Offrandes*, p. 5). In the N.K. this operation, usually called *st* (*set*, with), is often styled *st ḥr ḫnti* (*set her khenti*), "pouring in (or with?) *khenti*" (see Schiap., *L. dei F.*, Pl. xiii., l. 24, Text, ii., p. 171; with variants, *l.c.*, p. 314, and Mar., *Ab.*, i., Pl. xxxix*a.*), where , var. , &c., is evidently the name of the rite performed with these four vessels, and must mean literally "the first or opening ceremony." Hence the value of the sign.

Fig. 141. Globular water-pot; in the present instance coloured blue. In O.K. it is coloured red, with the upper part black (cf.). It appears in , and probably also in . In the offering of water and wine to the gods it was used in pairs, .

The sign indicates the contents of the vessel rather than the vessel itself. Thus , ,

&c., indicate the cosmic waters, i.e. the god *Nw* (*Nu*). Perhaps it is from this word that the single ʘ has its common phonetic value 𓈖𓅱 *nw* (*nu*), for which ʘʘʘ is preferred or often used in certain words, *mnw*, "monument," *Tḥnw*, "Libyan," while there are indications in 𓏏 (*q.v.*), and elsewhere, of the value *n* alone for ʘ. In the name of the goddess ʘ𓏏, ʘ𓏏𓇯, ʘʘ𓏏𓇯 (all in *Pyr.*), usually called Nut, the value of ʘ is not well defined, and may be *nn·t*, as the name of the goddess of the upper sky seems hardly distinguishable, except by tricks of writing, from that of the goddess of the sky in the lower hemisphere (*v.* ⊗). Maspero holds that the variant ʘʘ𓏏 𓇯, common in *Pyr.*, indicates *Nw·it*, by a pseudo-dual. In M.K., ʘ𓈖𓈖, and perhaps ʘ𓈖𓈖𓈖, stand for 𓅓𓐍𓈖 *m ḫn* (*m chen*), "inside" (*B. H.*, i., Pls. xxv., xxvi., ll. 193, 204, 215), and for *ymi ḫn* (*l.c.*, l. 209). In N.K., after the XVIIIth Dyn., 𓅓 is usually written before this group, and in late documents we often have 𓅓ʘ𓈖, 𓅓ʘ𓈖𓈖 for *m ḫn* (Piehl, *Ä. Z.*, 1887, 32, &c.). Thus it is probable that in 𓄡ʘ, *Pyr.* 𓐍𓈖ʘ *ḫn*, ʘ is really a word-sign.

Probably ʘ also represents a cooking-pot, 𓍑𓅓𓍑𓅓𓅱 *z'z'·w* (*zaza·u*), whence it commonly occurs even in O.K. in the group 𓋴𓋴ʘ𓏏, with various meanings. In 𓊽ʘ "grind," it seems to indicate a connexion with cookery. In 𓆰ʘ𓏏 perhaps it indicates the adaptation of rush baskets and mats to kitchen purposes (*v.* 𓆰). It is a peculiarity of the sign ʘ that it is used superfluously, in transference from any of the above groups where it would be a false det., and in the group 𓈖𓅱ʘ *nw*, where it only repeats the 𓅱.

𓏁 **Fig. 132.** A vase (here of the form *nems*) with water pouring from it.

This signifies both the action of purifying, 𓂝𓃀 *ʿb*, and the thing that is purified, 𓅱𓂝𓃀 *wʿb*. In *Pyr.* the spelling of these two words is variable, and sometimes there seems to be confusion between them. 𓂝 is there used as syl. for *ʿb* in either group. But after O.K. 𓏁 stands for the word *ʿb* only, and 𓃂 is *wʿb*, "pure," "priest," with little variation.

𓏏 **Figs. 40, 133.** Globular vase-shaped object suspended from a loop. The vase is surrounded at its widest part by a broad band of net-work (erased? in fig. 133). The band of net-work is one of the things which distinguish the vase determinative and symbolical of milk. In O.K. forms the vase is less globular, 𓏏, more like the milk vases offered in the temple-scenes, e.g. L., *D.*, iii., 20*c*. The teat or feeder (?) of the milk vase 𓏏, is, however, always absent from the sign 𓏏. In *Paheri*, Pl. iv., we see 𓏏 suspended round the neck of the infant prince Uazmes, who sits on the knees of his "nurse" and tutor, the nobleman Paheri.

The value of 𓏏 is 𓅓𓂋 *mr*, changing so early to 𓅓𓇋 *my* (*mȧ*), and 𓅓 *m*, on account of its weak terminal *r*, that its normal value may be said to be 𓅓𓇋 *my* (*mȧ*); the *r* in fact is quite lost after the O.K., even when 𓏏 occurs as the initial phon. of a word. In *Pyr.*, 𓏏, "like," is constantly written 𓅓𓏏𓂋 *mr*, but later it is 𓏏𓇋 *my* (*mȧ*). 𓉐, 𓅓[𓂋] *m*[*r*], varies with 𓅓 and 𓏏 in 𓉐𓏏𓎛𓏏, 𓅓[𓂋]𓎛𓂝𓏏 *m*[*r*]*ḥʿ·t* (*me*[*r*]*ḥȧ·t*), "tomb," and in 𓉐𓋴𓏏, 𓅓[𓂋]𓋴𓏏, *m*[*r*]*s·t*, "liver."

The milk vase, used as det. of the name of milk, depicted in the milk-offerings in the temples, and borne as his symbol on the head of a god tending the baby queen at Deir el Bahri (*D. el B.*, ii., Pl. liii.), was named 𓌻ʘ *mr*, as may be seen from 𓇋𓂋𓏏𓏏𓌻ʘ *yrṯ·t mr* (*ȧrthet mer*) (*Pyr. N.*, l. 258), "a *mr* vessel of milk." It may also be seen from the fact that in *Pyr.* the milk vessel 𓏏, with variant forms, is used as phon. in writing the word *mr*, "love," thus: , , , , &c. The appendage at the mouth of the vessel is apparently a flexible teat or feeder for artificially suckled infants and animals. Possibly, for superstitious reasons, fresh milk was by preference drawn through such a "teat." The projections at the side of the teat which we see in some instances, were probably intended for the child to hold, and the network band—as on —also was intended in all probability to prevent its slipping from the grasp; this may, however, turn out to be the fastening of the teat to the vessel.

Whether the was an amulet or plaything of leather or other soft material, or actually a feeding-bottle to hang round the neck, certainly to some extent it represents a milk vase, and its name is identical with that of the milk vase. As a nursery word it would be likely to lose the final *r* earlier than the same word used for the ordinary milk vessel.

Fig. 181. A bowl of red pottery (?), tied over and sealed at the top.

Word-sign for *ydr* (*ȧdr*), a word applied to cattle and birds of all domestic sorts; see examples, LORET, *Rec. de Trav.*, xviii., p. 205 *et seqq.* It is opposed to , *šd* (*shed*), "fatted up," in the case of birds (L., *D.*, iii., 30 *b*, l. 32). In *Kah. Pap.*, Pl. xvi., ll. 13, 14, *ydr* includes "draught oxen," as well as food-stock. *Ydr* therefore seems to be the ordinary stock or herds of cattle, geese, &c., that have not been specially fatted; it may thus be an expression for "domesticated" cattle and birds in general, as opposed to the wild cattle, antelopes, and birds. One writer considers that the select breeding stock is specially denoted by the word, but the passages quoted in his paper do not well bear this out, nor does the name *ydr* seem to point to it.

Possibly the sign may be connected with the preservation of meat in jars, certainly a practice in Ancient Egypt; or possibly with the food used for oxen. But it may be that the word *ydr*, as used in connexion with animals, has no pictorial relation to the hieroglyph; cf. *ydr·t*, *Pyr. N.*, l. 772, the peculiar det. of which may be the ancient form of this sign.

Fig. 154. Ring-stand for a jar, coloured red or white (L., *D.*, ii., 20), and flat or curved below. In the tomb of Tehutihetep, *nś·t*, "seat," is distinguished from *g*, which has a flat base (*El B.*, i., Pl. xxxi.). In N.K. the signs for *g* and *nś·t* and *dšr·t* (see below) all have the rounded base, and appear to be indistinguishable (for the first two see L., *D.*, iii., 59, *a*). In the early period likewise they are indistinguishable, and all *flat* below. Always they have a rim at the top, often also a rim below; sometimes the triangular opening seems to be absent. In *Medum*, Pl. xiii., below the table of offerings, the hole is at the top in *g*. (For *g*, see *Ptahhetep*, xli.; *Methen*, L., *D.*, ii., 5; for *nś·t*, *Ptahhetep*, xxxii.) Very rarely there seems to be (by confusion with ?) a raised edge all round (see L., *D.*, ii., 80, *d*, for *g*, and L., *D.*, ii., 64, *a* for *nś·t*). must be a ring-stand. In the sculptures and paintings, tall bases of tables, and stands for jars (like elongated), generally have the triangular hole, but this is very seldom seen in the shorter forms; examples may be found in L., *D.*, ii., 68, 101*b*, 104*c*. In L., *D.*, ii., 36, these stands are pierced both at top and at bottom.

Word-sign for:

1. *nś·t*. This apparently is not known as the name of a jar-stand, but is used in the figurative sense of "seat," "throne," "position" of a person, as transferable to his son.

2. *dšr·t* (*desher·t*). It is strange that the name of the *dšr·t* vase, which is shaped more or less as , is determined by ; that , is often the spelling of the name; and that represents the vase itself in tables of offerings and in scenes of offering; e.g., L., *D.*,

iii., 19*b*. We can, however, find a partial explanation in the fact that the two vases often used together, *nms·t* and *dšr·t*, have each the same form (LEPS., *Ä. T.*, 43) in the lists, and also where the vase is represented actually in use, being emptied over statue or person (ROS., *M. del C.*, lx.; cf. *D. el B.*, i., Pl. xi., in which the vase is unfortunately destroyed). In order to mark a distinction between these two important kinds of ceremonial vases, the Egyptians represented the *nms·t* vase by a picture of itself, and the *dšr·t* vase by . Probably such a stand was practically always of pottery, and thus implied red pottery, which was presumably the distinguishing characteristic of *dšr·t*, "the red" vase, in its ancient form. But in *Leyd. Mon.*, iii., 24, the is actually of silver, and bronze is generally represented by red colour.

3. Alph. for *g*, and phon. for *g*ʾ (*ga*). The origin of this value is to be found, on the analogy of *dšr·t*, in the name ▽ (*Pyr. P.*, l. 707), a vessel the shape of which is presumably shown by the det. The word is frequently found later for a cup or bowl on which fruits were placed, and as denoting a drinking-bowl it is the origin of the Coptic ϫⲱ, ϫⲟⲓ, a "drinking-bowl" or "cup." See also △.

To sum up: the ring-stand (1) was probably named *nś·t*, "stand," which word is often found in the meaning of "throne," "seat." It was essentially a pottery form, and though occasionally made in more valuable material, it was generally of red or other coarse pottery, being pretty well hidden from view by the vessel standing upon it. In this way (2) it symbolized the red pottery (?) *dšr·t* vase, , in order to distinguish it from the *nms·t* vase, which was of the same form, but presumably of different material; and (3) it symbolized the pottery (?) *g*ʾ vase, ▽, shaped ▽, in order to distinguish it from other sorts, such as , , &c., made probably of basket-work, wood, metal, &c. From this last use it obtains the alphabetic value *g*, as well as its biliteral value *g*ʾ (*ga*).

In *Ptahhetep*, Pl. xxxvi. 3, there seems to be an instance of used as det. of *f*ʾ (*fa*), "carry," "support," usually .

▽ [*B. H.*, iii., fig. 34, cf. fig. 62.] Cup, of wood (?).

Name, *ḥn·t*. Word-sign for *ḥn·t* (1) as the name of this cup, used for liquids in offerings (*B. H.*, iii., p. 15), and (2) as word for "mistress," probably having the same radical meaning (cf. , p. 47). A similar vessel is named "handful," hence in the base period the alph. value of ▽.

Word-sign for *wśḫ* (*uśekh*), "width," probably by reference to the "diameter" of the circular vessel seen in elevation; with rad. ext.

Word-sign in N.K. for *ʿb* (*ȧb*), perhaps through the word , later , "an offering," offerings being commonly represented in vessels ▽.

Fig. 145. Potter's kiln; for scenes in which the kiln is depicted see *El B.*, i., Pl. xxvii. 2, and p. 34; *B. H.*, i., Pl. xi., &c.

Word-sign for , *t*ʾ (*ta*), "fervent heat," whence it is phon. for *t*ʾ, usually written . This group must not be confounded with , , *v.* .

[*B. H.*, iii., fig. 85.] Flame from a brazier, with falling smoke and soot (?), often of the form . Both forms of the vessel containing the fire are found amongst the dets. of the word *ʿḫ* (*ȧkh*), "brazier," in *Pyr.* (*M.*, l. 239; *N.*, l. 616, &c.).

Word-sign—rarely used by itself—for *psf* or *pfs*, "cook"; *śrf*, "heat" *v.* ; more often for "brazier," "censer," "flame," *Mentuhotep*, p. 24.

Det. of heat, fire, &c.

Fig. 70. Censer with a flame, or small cloud of smoke rising from it. The flame is usually represented with a pointed tip. It occurs often as , with two balls of incense. Perhaps the sign is not found at all before the N.K. It is, however, figured in *Mentuhotep*, Pl. iv., with the name , *šz·t*, "censer."

In N.K. the figure occurs, often with a taller flame, as id. or symbol, probably for the expression "incense upon a burning censer" (e.g. *Paheri*, Pl. v., right edge, 2nd row). Det. of *š·ntr*, "incense" (*Methen*, L., *D.*, ii., 3). In the earliest inscriptions the word for incense is usually spelt , as if *št ntr* (*šeth neter*), "divine perfume," but subsequent variants of O.K. and later, show that this is really a peculiar writing of the causative *š·ntr*, lit. "making" or "made divine."

In good writing occurs otherwise only in the groups , , , each of which means "soul," and is to be read *b'* (*ba*). In *Pyr.* the name of the "soul," usually written , is sometimes written , (for variant forms see *P.*, ll. 270, 416). In these groups evidently corresponds to , and so is probably a censer or brazier; it also occurs in *b'·t*, *P.*, l. 615. (Note that in *Pyr.* there is frequently found a verb *b'*, meaning "to possess soul-power," "to be as a soul.")

In the usual groups for *b'*, "soul," viz. O. and M.K., N.K. (early), and (XIXth Dynasty, &c.), it is clear that , lit. "digger," is only used for the soul by phon. trans., and that was added as a determinative or a distinctive word-sign ideographic of the soul (as the power of flame); a still clearer definition was obtained by substituting for the picture-form of a human soul as a human-headed hawk, ; or , the embodiment of the "soul of Osiris" in the ram of Mendes.

K. Fibres, Textiles; Basket-, Mat-, and Leather-Work.

Fig. 124. Hank of fibres (of flax?) in the form of a loop thrice twisted, and with the ends loose. In the fine sculpture of Usertesen I. (*Koptos*, Pl. ix.), on the original, this sign is clearly represented as composed of a number of parallel stems or fibres. The hank is twisted as if being wrung to dry it, doubtless after the work of beating and cleansing in water was completed. In fig. 124 it is coloured green, as being of vegetable material; in *Medum* it is yellow. Parallel changes of colour are found throughout the rope and rush series of hieroglyphs.

The form of the sign, and the existence of a verb , *ḥ*, "beat," suggests that represents flax fibres "beaten" out, a process which is probably shown in *B. H.*, i., Pl. xi., 5th row; *B. H.*, ii., Pl. iv., 2nd row; Pl. xiii., 2nd row, the last representation being the best (the inscription reads *qnqn nw·t*, "beating threads, or fibres"). It may perhaps be questioned whether the name of flax, , *mḥ*, (with , det. of the cubit which has the same sound) is not a derivative from *ḥ*, "strike." *v.* also .

From the above word-sign value is derived its alphabetic value , *ḥ*.

Cf. Fig. 86. Coil of rope.

(1) Symbol for the numeral 100. The general name for rope is , *nwḥ*, applied often to rope used in field measurement (Bon., *Sarc.*, Pl. vi.). The standard in linear field measurement was a rope of 100 cubits, and evidently this was the standard length in rope manufacture. This length was called , *ḫt* (*khet*), "stick," or more fully, *ḫt n nwḥ*, "a stick of rope." The *arura*, 100 cubits square, is named "a stretch (of the rope)"—a depth of 100 cubits from the frontage being always assumed (cf. *P. S. B. A.*,

xiv., 417 *et seqq.*). Hence, on account of its standard length, , a rope, is the sign for 100, which in Egyptian is named *š·t* (*she·t*) (Sethe, *Ä. Z.*, 1893, 112), and hence the value *š* (*sh*) for , which Piehl has identified in Ptolemaic texts (*Actes VIII. Congr. Stockholm*, p. 10).

(2) Word-sign for *šn·t* (*shen·t*), *v.* .

(3) The value *w* (*u*) for which this sign stands in N.K. as a substitute for , is difficult to account for. By some it is supposed to be derived from a hieratic form of somewhat resembling that for ; it may be partly due to words like , *w'w'* (*uaui*), and , *w'r* (*uar*), "cord." At that time the advantage of possessing alternative letters for forming hieroglyphic groups was strongly felt, though most of the new values did not enter into hieratic writing until a very late period. In this way the horizontal (properly, *ym* (*ȧm*)) was used for , and were equated with , with , and with . for *w* seems even to occur in *Pyr. W.*, l. 215, for *ywr* (*ȧur*).

Det. of names of rope and of words indicating its use.

Fig. 180; *B. H.*, iii., fig. 51. Cord wound on stick. A fine example is in *Ptahhetep*, Pl. xxxiii., top, 3rd col. from left; see also L., *D.*, ii., 97*b*.

Word-sign for *wz* (*uz*), "stick or hank of cord"; see *B. H.*, iii., p. 19.

Phon. for .

Fig. 86. Coil of rope across a stick. Borchardt (*Ä. Z.*, 1897, p. 105) considers that this sign represents a bolt, , with the cord for drawing it from the outside when it was fixed inside. An example copied by Miss Paget in the tomb of Rekhmara shows the clearly, but this form is perhaps not ancient, and may be only a N.K. invention connected with the phonetic value of supplying the *s* in *st'* and *'s* (*v.* Addenda).

Word-sign for *st*, later *st'*, "haul," with phon. trans.

Det. of *'s* (*as*), "hasten," often transitive as if "to pull" or "drag on." This word does not occur in O.K., unless it be in the form of the intransitive verb , var. , "pass on."

Figs. 41, 43. Rope arranged in a loop; at one end a noose, the other end is turned down at a sharp angle, the tip pointed and in it (fig. 41) a narrow slit or noose in the substance of the rope. On M.K. coffins this object is figured with, or near to, weapons (*Mentuhotep*, Pls. iii., v., and p. 18; *Ä. T.*, 38, &c.); the form varies: sometimes there is a noose at one or other end only (fig. 43); sometimes we have , with a clear loop at each end (*Mentuhotep*, Pl. iii.), but this is not a hieroglyph.

On the coffins the name is *rz*; *rwz* (*ruz*). This name is met with in *Pyr. N.*, l. 975, apparently denoting the loops or knots used in the construction of a ladder. In *Kah. Pap.*, i., l. 5, it seems to stand for a bow-string, or better, a lasso; in Bon., *Sarc.*, Pl. iv. d., l. 21, the word in the plural signifies the "bonds" of captives by which their arms were tied behind their backs, . Clearly the proper sense of the sign is a noosed or knotted rope. It has been supposed to represent a sling, but of this there is no clear evidence; sometimes it may represent a halter. (Slingers are mentioned in *Piankhy*, l. 32, and in *B. H.*, ii., Pl. xv., one slinger seems to be figured; but they are rarely found on Egyptian monuments.)

Hence phon. for .

Word-sign for *'r* (*ar*), and *'yr* (*aȧr*), "oppress." Other words of this form spelt with , e.g. *m'r* (*mar*), "poor," "feeble"; *š'r* (*šar*), "poor"; *d'yr*, *dy'r*, "restrain," generally have the notion of constraint in one form or other, and are probably all derivatives of *y'r*, *'yr*. In *Siut*, Tomb I., l. 350, &c., [hieroglyphs] stands for [hieroglyphs] *d'yr srf* (*daär serf*), "restrain hot temper"; cf. SH., *Eg. Ins*, i., 83, l. 11.

[hieroglyph] Fig. 128. A cord, coloured green (so also L., *D.*, ii., 90), arranged at one end in two loops, apparently for a slip-knot of a special kind (with a bow at the side), of which the detail is never fully shown. In the present example there is also a slight projection at the other end of the cord, no doubt to mark the fraying.

Phon. for [hieroglyphs] *w'* (*ua*). There are two words that may be connected with it, viz. (1) [hieroglyphs] (*Pyr. T.*, l. 178, &c.), [hieroglyphs] *w'w'* (*uaua*), meaning perhaps "cord of foundation," and "to bind together." (2) [hieroglyphs], [hieroglyphs] *w'r* (*uar*), "measuring cord," "cord." The latter might conceivably be the origin of the phon. value through loss of the final *r*, but more probably *w'* is here the simplified form of *w'w'* (cf. pp. 4, 5).

[hieroglyph] [*B. H.*, iii., fig. 78.] Loop of cord. [hieroglyph] is a debased form, derived from the M.K. cursive hieratic form for [hieroglyph] used in late N.K. hieratic for [hieroglyph].

Word-sign for [hieroglyphs] *šn* (*shen*), "surround," "encircle," so perhaps a "loop." After O.K. *šn·t* is usually written [hieroglyph].

Phon. for *šn*.

[hieroglyph] Fig. 134; *B. H.*, iii., fig. 22. Short cord ending in small loops, apparently a handle for drawing or dragging. The sign is often represented as a twisted cord; here it is green, but in *Medum* (Pls. xi., xii.) yellow.

In *Pyr. T.*, l. 308, is a word [hieroglyphs] *ṯṯ·t* (*theth·t*), for a binding or catching cord, there used as a weapon against a serpent, but perhaps also the name of the cord in the sign [hieroglyph], the phonetic value of which would be reduced from it to *ṯ* (*th*) by the usual simplifying process, see pp. 4, 5. The corresponding verb [hieroglyphs] *ṯṯ*, is regularly written [hieroglyph], cf. [hieroglyph].

[hieroglyph] Fig. 111. Rope-knot with four loops at each side and one at each end.

Word-sign for [hieroglyphs] *s'* (*sa*), "guard," "protect," convertible with [hieroglyph] in the sense of "amulet"; in *Pyr.* a common word-sign for the verb "to protect," &c., but in later times confined to the substantival sense "amulet," "protection." It is probably a magic knot, but may represent a particularly secure way of tying up a packet with a number of cross-strings.

[hieroglyph] Fig. 130. Thread-line, curved down to show its flexibility. In *Medum*, *passim*, and *B. H.*, iii., fig. 25, [hieroglyph] is coloured red, and once in *Medum* (Pl. xi.) yellow. The picture of the object is seen in [hieroglyph], id. of cloth and det. of words of similar meaning. Cf. also [hieroglyph]. In *Horhotep* (*Miss. Arch.*, i., Pl. xiii.), balls of yarn or bundles of cloth are tied with [hieroglyph]. Cords hanging over stretched lines are represented as [hieroglyph].

Alph. for *ś* = Heb. שׂ. The distinction between [hieroglyph] and [hieroglyph] was not observed in writing after O.K. It seems likely that [hieroglyph] obtained its value *ś* from the suffixes of the fem. pronoun *ś*, *śi*, owing to thread and cloth working of all kinds being a woman's occupation. In "sportive" hieroglyphs [hieroglyph] takes the place of [hieroglyph].

[hieroglyph] Fig. 53. Apparently a number of threads, regularly spaced, each looped at one end, and at the other attached to a horizontal bar of wood; a thread passes through the loops parallel to the bar, and from near one end of the latter there projects a short curved handle (?). The number of threads varies from four to five; they are perhaps never at right angles to the bar, which seems as if it might be either drawn along, or pushed back by the handle. The O.K.

form appears to have been different, but there is no trustworthy example to quote. The sign suggests a connexion with weaving, especially with the weaver's "heald" (for drawing down or lifting a certain number of the warp threads in the loom, and thus affording passage for the shuttle); but the "heald" would show a separate thread through each loop, the threads would be vertical and the handle different. It seems as though there were some connexion between the number of threads and the number of fingers —4, or of fingers and thumb—5. In the numerous examples of the XVIIIth Dyn. the most usual number seems 4, though 5 is not uncommon. In L., *D.*, ii., 123*f*, there is an abnormal form composed of the four fingers, , crossed by the arm, , and evidently indicating the four digits of the palm-measure, *šsp*.

Word-sign for "palm" of the hand, , *šsp* (*s͟hesep*), or *šp* (*s͟hep*), lit. "the receiver," "holder"; also for the verb *šsp*, "receive," "hold." After O.K. the sign was transferred to words originally spelt *sšp* (*ses͟hep*).

Figs. 26, 114. A roll of yellow cloth (for bandaging ?), the lower part bound or laced over, the upper end appearing as a flap at the top, probably for unwinding. Cf. *B. H.*, iii., p. 25. On M.K. coffins (e.g. *Mentuhotep*) this symbol figures among the supplies; in some such cases (e.g. *Sebekaa*) the upright part appears to be arranged lengthwise in a hank, not rolled. In N.K. hatchets were made which in outline resemble this figure, perhaps intentionally. It is possible, indeed, that the present object represents a fetish, e.g. a bone carefully wound round with cloth, and not the cloth alone; but this idea is not as yet supported by any ascertained facts.

On the coffins the name is , , *nṯr* (*net͟her*), meaning probably "divine" cloth; the same name occurs commonly in the earliest tables of offerings (*Medum*, xiii., xvi., xx.). By rad. ext. it expresses *nṯr*, "god," "divine," in which sense it is exceedingly common from the earliest times; gradually it became det. of divine names and id. of divinity, but was very rarely so used in O.K. It should be noted that in O.K. the proper id. of "god," the word-sign for *nṯr*, the det. of divinity and of the names of individual gods, was , the sacred hawk on its perch, (*q.v.*), and thus distinguished from its wild congeners.

Figs. 61, 160. Perhaps a pleated cloth or article of dress running on a tape or string, the two looped (?) ends of which are spread out. The pleats shown vary in number; cf. *Methen*, L., *D.*, ii., 7*b*, for a good outline showing nine pleats. , *ym'ḫ* (*ȧmak͟h*), is essentially the same object as that represented by , but it has only one looped (?) end. The meaning of *ym'ḫ* is retirement in old age with honourable ease after a life of faithful service. This seems to be symbolized in a remarkable manner by the pleated cloth , drawn together and folded to be put away. Perhaps this cloth, or article of apparel, was ceremonial, and after use was folded over, and so kept in "easy and honourable retirement" in perpetuity. In *Medum*, Pl. xiii., has as many as ten pleats, indicating that in all they were very numerous.

The usual meaning of , *'w* (*au*), as a word-sign is "stretch out," "open out," "length," apparently as opposed to , the pleats also indicating that it was capable of great extension.

Phon. for *'w* (*au*). The controversy as to the phonetic value of this sign has been summed up by W. Max Müller, *P. S. B. A.*, xviii., 187 *et seqq.* The supposed value *fw* (*fu*) does not seem to have existed in early times.

[*B. H.*, i., Pl. xxvii.] Ball of rush-work (?). In O.K. yellow, with horizontal reeding (*Medum*, *passim*, &c.); later green, and generally with oblique reeding (*El B.*, i., *passim*, &c.).

Alph. for *ḫ* (*kh*). being phon. for *ḫw* (*khu*) in O.K. (cf. SETHE, *Ä. Z.*, 1897, 6), this points to *ḫ* (*kh*) being the name or proper value of . It may be connected with *ḫiḫi* (*khikhi*), "toss up," or with *ḫḫ* or *ḫʾḫ* (*khakh*), "run swiftly."

Cf. Fig. 22. Bowl or basket of rush-work, without handle; in early examples yellow, indicating the dry rushes of which it was composed, and generally showing the horizontal reeding (L., *D.*, ii., 20); later green.

Name, , *nb·t*, "holder," preserved only in one passage of *Pyr. M.*, l. 238 = *N.*, l. 616, already referred to *s.v.* (*q.v.*); with rad. ext. and phon. trans. as in *nb*, "master," "holder," "possessor," and *nb*, "swim."

Fig. 92. *Neb*-basket (*q.v.*), with loop handle outside, below the rim. The distinctive loop is often omitted in *Pyr.*, probably by inadvertence. Colouring, &c., as , *Medum*, Pls. xviii., xxiv.

Alph. for *k*. In a very late text there is a plant-name *kk* (*kek*), believed by LORET (*Rec. de Trav.*, v., 87) to mean a "rush," which thus might be connected with the value *k* of the basket . More probably this *k* is from a root *kʾ*, "work" (*v.*). In O.K. *kʾ* is commonly written ; a basket is necessary to every workman's outfit, and in Egypt would be especially appropriate as a symbol of labour.

Fig. 95. This picture evidently represents mat-work made of reeds tied together. It may, however, not be a simple mat, which was usually represented oblong, as in ; in *Medum*, Professor Petrie calls it a bundle (?). Colouring as in .

Alph. for *p*. There is a rare word, , *p* (SCHÄFER, *Ä. Z.*, 1897, 98), meaning a "stand," "base," on which a thing may stand—an article of temple furniture—whether of wood or stone, according to the det. Perhaps the word meant originally a mat or stand of basket-work, and was the name of the object , but it is now only known from late texts. The ancient city *P*, lay in the marshes of the Delta, where mat-working may have been much practised.

Fig. 94. A reed mat, on which is placed a loaf of bread as an offering. The colour of the mat (in contrast to that of , &c.) is green or blue-green from the earliest times, presumably because it was made of freshly-gathered stems (*Medum*, Pl. xiii.; L., *D.*, ii., 19).

The name of an offering is *ḥtp* (*ḥetep*), lit. "propitiation," "peace"; and this sign is the word-symbol for *ḥtp* in all its meanings.

Cf. Fig. 13. Loop formed of a band of springy reeds (?), bent round, and the ends lashed together in such a way as to make a straight base. Colouring as in , L., *D.*, ii., 20.

Word-sign for *šnnw*, *šnw* (*shennu*, *shenu*), "circle," "ring," also a "great multitude." The "cartouche," , named also *šnnw* (SCHÄFER, *Ä. Z.*, 1896, 167), is of precisely the same construction as , but elongated for the reception of the signs composing the king's name (cf. SETHE, *Ä. Z.*, 1897, p. 4). In this it may indicate a protective ring keeping off the profane; cf. its use in N.K. as det. of *šnʿ* (*shenā*), "hinder," "obstruct."

Fig. 23. Two bundles of reeds or rushes (?) tied together at the top and spreading out downwards; near the lower ends they are loosely connected by a cord. In the early period (in *Pyr.*) this sign seems to be very variable. It may possibly represent a straw cap used in stoppering and sealing wine-jars.

Word-sign for *zbʾ* (*zeba*), which has

various meanings, "block up," "covering," "exchange," &c.

 **Fig. 82**; *B. H.*, iii., fig. 27. Bag or pouch (of leather ?) tied and sealed; used for precious metals, powders for the toilet, &c. It occurs in composition as id. or det. of toilet powders. The present example is of the regular form in O.K. (e.g. *Medum*, Pl. xiii., lower left) and in N.K. In M.K. it is often , perhaps the same thing opened, showing strap and loop for fastening. Prof. Maspero mentions having found leathern bags like tobacco pouches, fastened with a lace, containing eye-paint; these were from (prehistoric ?) tombs at Gebelên. The scribe-artists always distinguish it from the loop of rope,  *šs* (*shes*), though that occasionally has a looped end,  (*Medum*, Pl. xiii., lower right).

The name of the bag or pouch is *ʿrf* (*ȧrf*), of which word this sign is det., with rad. ext.; but in a number of place-names it has the value *g*, viz.  *Gbtiw* (*Gebtiu*), Coptos (*Koptos*, Pl. vi. *et seqq.*);  (*Paheri*, Pl. viii., cornice line, from which the present example is taken), variant 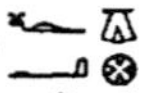 *Fʿg* (*Fȧg*), Eileithyiapolis;  *Gsm*, Goshen. Some of these names are probably not pure Egyptian, but suggestive of foreign origin, and the value of  is often rather *q* than  *g*. One may perhaps connect this value with the idea of tight packing, compression,  *gʾ* (*ga*).

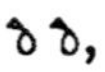, the same sign doubled, may represent the two bags of the two kinds of eye-paint, *mesdem* and *uaz*, or may be simply intensive of the idea of compression. It occurs in the place-name 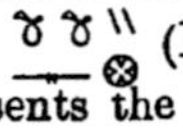 (Br., *D. G.*, 864), where perhaps it represents the above *g*, but is doubled to distinguish it from the group  *šs* (originally *šś*, *šś·t*), "alabaster."

Word-sign for  or 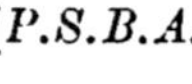 *wgʾ* (*uga*), "helplessness," "weakness" (*P.S.B.A.*, xiii., 74). In *Medum*, Pl. xvii., lower right, it occurs in a proper name.

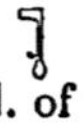 **Fig. 27.** Roll of sacred linen, with bag id. of toilet powders.

Graphic compound; the name of a sacred cleansing powder or earth. Early variants of the sign (cf. e.g. *Pyr. M.*, l. 28, with parallel passages) give  *nṯr*, alone, which is therefore the name of the substance contained in the bag. This was probably natron, or perhaps nitre. The Greek name *νίτρον* is derived from the Ancient Egyptian. In many forms of *nṯr* the final *r* was lost, but apparently it was retained in this word.

L. Implements, Tools.

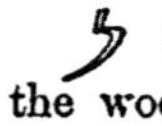 **Figs. 33, 113.** Sickle set with flints, the wood coloured green. Cf. *Kahun*, ix., 22; *Illahun*, vii., 27. For the unexplained green colour, which is constant in all representations, see Spurrell in *T. el A.*, pp. 37, 38; cf. also *Medum*, frontispiece; *B. H.*, i., Pl. xxvii.

Det. of  *ʾsḫ* (*asekh*), "reap." The name of the sickle is 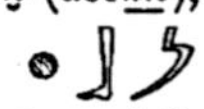 *ḫb* (*kheb*), or possibly ,  *ḫʾb* (*chab*), "the curved." Word-sign and phon. for  *mʾ* (*ma*)—varying to  *ʾm* (*am*).  = 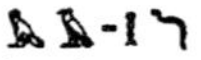 *mʾ-ḥz* (*maḥez*), "the white *ma* (?)," is the oryx, possibly in reference to its curved horns (?).  "lion," and ,  *šmʾ* (*śma*), "slaughter"—perhaps the causative of a word *mʾ*—may point to the origin: but this is mere conjecture. Can it be connected with  "grasp"?

 **Fig. 117.** Wooden hand-hoe, made of a long bent blade held in place by a cord attached to the handle.

The hoe was called  *ḥnn* (*Pyr. M.*, l. 696, &c.), especially in its simplest form, made with

a forked branch, (*Medum*, Pl. xv.). apparently owed its common word-sign value *mr* to being made of two pieces "bound" together, from , *mr*, "bind." Rarely used as phon.

Det. of hoeing, hacking, &c.

Fig. 186. Piece of grained wood with a loop or handle on one side in the middle of its length. In *Methen* (L., *D.*, ii., 7*b*) the loop is below the middle. It may very well represent a plasterer's "float" or smoothing board. The type commonly used in print for *qd* is quite wrong, though in very late texts the sign is conventionalized to nearly this form.

Word-sign for *qd* (*qed*), "build," "shape," &c.; with phon. trans.

Fig. 80. Chisel, consisting of a tongue-shaped metal blade set in a stout wooden handle. This is a chisel to be driven by a mallet. In *Medum*, frontispiece, fig. 17, and Pl. xi., the handle is cylindrical (with strengthening bands). It appears to be distinct from the awl worked by the bow-drill, the handle of the awl being more slender.

The name of the object is , *mnḫ* (*me<u>nkh</u>*) (*Leyd. Mons.*, iii., 24; *Tomb. Sety I.*, Part iii., Pl. xiii.), and the sign is used as general word-symbol for *mnḫ*.

Fig. 107. Pointed instrument with wooden handle of peculiar shape showing that it is to be worked by hand; cf. *Medum*, Pls. xviii., xxiv., and p. 32. On a VIth Dynasty O.K. stela in the old Bulak Museum the sign has the chisel end in a handle of rushes (?) bound together. The form also seems fairly well authenticated (L., *D.*, ii., 121). Apparently it is a chisel or borer to be worked by hand, not struck with the hammer. For such use the handle might well be of softer material, and being constructed by binding the tool may hence have received its name; cf. .

Word-sign for *mr*, used also in the pseudo-causative *šmr*, "royal friend." The "sportive" hieroglyph of *B. H.*, iii., fig. 80, standing for *mr sm·wt* (*mer sem·ut*), "governor of the desert," shows that *mr* is a word connected with drilling or piercing, but the present sign can hardly be a tool for working with a bow-drill.

Figs. 20, 96; *B. H.*, iii., fig. 89. Drill-cap (?), coloured greenish blue (in *B. H.*, iii., fig. 89, too green). In *Medum* it is black. In *Mentuhotep*, Pl. iv. ("*fuss-seite*"), and p. 28 = *Ä. T.*, Pl. 29, where the outlines of the group of tools are clearer, the object is figured along with tools—bow-drill, chisel, &c.—and coloured blue-green. Petrie's identification of the object as a black stone drill-cap seems more likely to prove correct than that of Steindorff as a polisher. The caps found with small drills are usually made of the hard dark *dôm*-nut, and are much more conical than , as indeed they are represented in scenes of carpentering, cf. *B. H.*, iii., fig. 80. But at Kahun, Petrie found black stone pivots or drill-caps, shaped roughly . In the scenes the polishing-stones are generally represented as white, and oblong or oval.

Whatever may be the object represented by this sign, its name seems to have been *yt* (*ảt*), with fugitive , rather than *t* alone. Compare its homophony as a word-sign with , *yt* (*ảt*), "loaf"; with , *yt* (*ảt*), "father," &c. Probably "drill-cap," , , "loaf," or cake of potter's clay on the wheel (*Pyr. P.*, 424 = *N.*, 1211), all bear the same name , owing to their more or less domed form.

As phon., loses the presumptive initial , and becomes alph. for *t*.

[Cf. *B. H.*, iii., fig. 73.] Adze with metal blade bound to wooden handle.

As an ordinary tool it is called *n·t* (*ȧn·t*), lit. "claw" (*Tomb. Sety I.*, Part iii., Pl. xiii., 2, right edge; and *Leyd. Mons.*, iii., Pl. xxiv., in lists of tools); hence, sometimes in *Pyr.* word-sign for this term in the sense of "claw." The sacred adzes used in the ceremony of "opening the mouth" are called simply (*Leyd. Mons.*, *l.c.*), or more particularly (var.) "the *nw* (*nu*) of Anubis" (M., *Ab.*, i., Pl. xxvi. *i*; SCHIAP., *L. d. F.*, i., pp. 104, 105). Hence phon. for *nw* (*nu*), usually written . In *Pyr.* sometimes det. of *nzr*, "cut with an adze."

[*B. H.*, iii., fig. 73.] Adze and piece of wood (grooved).

Word-sign for *śtp* (reason unknown), and often for *nw*. In the geographical name *ʿnp·t* (*Ȧnp·t*), i.e. Mendes, which is spelt with the adze, it is uncertain whether or is the more correct as word-sign. Cf. *Medum*, Pl. xxi., where the sign is perhaps injured, but seems to represent the handle only of the adze. The origin of this value is perhaps to be sought in local mythology.

[*B. H.*, iii., fig. 70.] Knife, coloured black. For this particular form cf. *B. H.*, iii., p. 38, Pl. ix., fig. 4, Pl. x., fig. 2. The example figured is taken from *B. H.*, i., Pl. xviii., where it is the name of a locality sacred to the goddess Pakhet, namely the ravine of Speos Artemidos, called in the N.K. inscriptions of that temple. In *B. H.*, i., Pl. xxiv., there is a variant , written with a peculiar animal. The reading is by no means certain.

The knife is word-sign for *dś*, "a knife," "blade," "sharp point"; with some rad. ext. (in *Pap. Eb.*). Cf. *Pyr. M.*, l. 352; in *Methen* (L., *D.*, ii., 13), the sign for *dś* is , apparently a harpoon-head with single barb. Word-sign also for "the sharp thing," "sword," "blade"—e.g. of an adze (*Leyd. Mons.*, iii., 24), in *Pyr. P.*, l. 81, &c., *dmᵓ·t*; cf. *Metternich Stela*, l. 82, where (i.e. *ḥri dm·t*) = in *Pap. Eb.*; with rad. ext. In *Pap. Eb.*, &c., there is a verb "cut away," "remove," which may be *św*ᵓ (*sua*), "cut away," "cut down." In *Pap. Eb.*, xci., 15, occurs a word "to lance (?)," which may be connected with *śfw*ᵓ, "knives" (*B. H.*, iii., p. 34); but the usual form, like that of the verb "to slaughter" oxen, is *śft*, with radical *t* (*v.* Addenda).

Det. of cutting, and cutting instruments.

[*B. H.*, iii., figs. 63, 65.] Knife or chopper in conical handle. In O.K. a straight-backed blade alone.

Word-sign for *nm*. *Nm·t* is the name of the executioner's block in Hades at which heads and limbs were lopped off; perhaps the same word, but written by a peculiar and variable id., is used for the butcher's block in *Pyr.*, where there is also a word *nm* found in connexion with the execution of the enemy of Osiris, *P.*, ll. 598, 600.

Phon. for *nm*.

Figs. 42, 129; *B. H.*, iii., figs. 64, 68. Fire-stick apparatus, in fig. 42 consisting of drill with two ridges—to prevent bow-string from slipping—standing on the matrix. In *B. H.*, iii., fig. 68, the drill is faceted, and there is also a groove for the bow-string to work in, when that was used. *B. H.*, iii., fig. 64, shows how the sticks were used and re-used as matrices. In *Medum*, Pl. xxviii., 1, the top of the drill has been charred by previous use of that end, and a drill-hole has also been burnt in it. The drills from Kahun (*Kahun*, p. 29, *Illahun*, p. 11; cf. *Ten Years' Diggings*, fig. 91) are composite, having separate stock, faceted like *B. H.*, iii., fig. 68, and capped with another piece of wood. In the hieroglyph , the drill is generally simple, but in fig. 129 it has more the appearance of the drill-head from a composite drill.

The value of  is 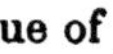 *s*ʾ (*za*). The blackened drill-holes seem unmistakable evidence as to the origin of this sign, and BORCHARDT (*Ä. Z.*, 1897, p. 105) accepts the solution. But the Egyptian name of the fire-drill is as yet unidentified, and it seems at present impossible to show the connexion of the value with fire-making.

 Fig. 174. The support of a balance, consisting of a post, from the upper part of which projects a curved peg; the lower end of the post is fixed in a firm base.

This object is named 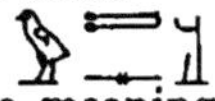 *wts* (*uthes*), "support," the word also meaning to "weigh" (in a balance). After O.K. it has two other values, (1) 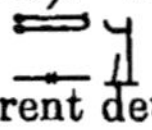 *ts* (*thes*), "raise" (in O.K. with a different det.), transferred also to other meanings; and (2) 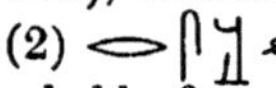 *rš*, "wake up," "be wakeful," probably from connexion of ideas with "rising," "being raised," and confusion with .

M. WAR, HUNTING, &c.

 Fig. 190. Conventionalized bow, or yoke for carrying. In the "prehistoric" sculpture (DE MORGAN, *Recherches*, ii., p. 265, better in *Rev. Arch.*, 1890, Pl. iv.) the bows are nearly of this type; later they are very different.

Word-sign for 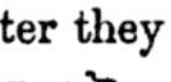 *pz·t*, "bow," lit. "the stretched," "stretcher," which might very well be also the name of the yoke. Used with phon. transf.

 [*B. H.*, iii., fig. 32.] Arrow.

Name, 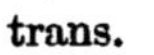 *ššr* (*shešer*), "arrow"; with phon. trans. Used also, even in O.K., for 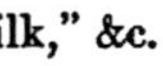 *ššr* (*šesher*), *šhr* (*šecher*), "to milk," &c. Word-sign for  *šwn* (*šun*), "physician," 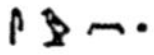 "price," &c. The name *swn*, for an arrow, is only found in very late mythological texts, and its authenticity as the origin of the value *šwn* may be doubted.

 Fig. 85. Mace, with nearly globular, or ovate white head, the handle crossed by a loop of cloth or cord. Compare *Medum*, p. 31, and *B. H.*, i., Pl. xxvii.

The mace with head of this form was called  *hz* (*hez*), "the white," or fem. ,  *hz·t* (*Mentuhotep*, p. 18, no. 8).

Word-sign for  *hz*; with phon. trans. The loop across it probably marks and defines the meaning "white," linen and clothing being usually of that colour; it may be added to distinguish  from  "green," and "string." The addition of the loop is found occasionally from the earliest times.

The mace is written with the phonetic complement thus, , , to distinguish it from  *wd*, "string," and 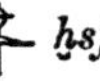 *hsf*.

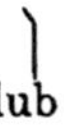 [*B. H.*, iii., fig. 77.] Curved or angulated club or throw-stick; its forms include the fowler's throw-stick (e.g. L., *D.*, ii., 130 = *B. H.*, i., Pl. xxxii., where the hieroglyph  immediately above the hand holding the stick reads *qm*ʾ).

The throwing club was the weapon of the desert tribes east and west of Egypt (cf. *B. H.*, i., Pls. xvi., bottom right, xxxi., xlv.), but not of the negroes, to judge by its use in O.K. writing. With the complement , thus, , it indicates the 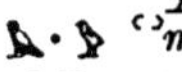 ʿʾ*m·w* (*Āamu*), or eastern Bedawîn, &c.; while with  *nw*, , it denotes the Libyans on the west, the 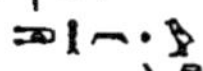 *thn·w* (*Tehen·u*); and in *Una*, l. 16, 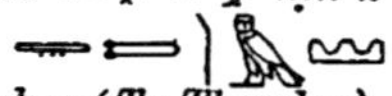 stands for  *t*ʾ *tmh·w* (*Ta Themh·u*), i.e. Libya. In the M.K. even the name of the negroes was written 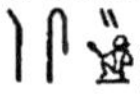, for [illegible] *nhši* (*Nehеši*), though earlier the [illegible] was not attached to this name in any form. Grouped [illegible],

, gradually it became det. for all names of foreign countries, cities, and tribes, and was used even for the frontier city of $\underline{T}$ʾ*rw*, "Zaru"; in O.K. its use as det. was very limited.

The variants of the group , in the lists of offerings, are confused, but early texts (e.g. *Ptahhetep*, Pl. xli.) point to being in this case = *qmʾ* (*qema*), a very common value of . In late times it was used as word-sign and phon. for in many words = , which is properly *gm*. As word-sign also it has the value *tn* (*then*). As word-sign for *qmʾ* it may express *creating in kinds*, in relation to races of men, since takes a leading place in the spelling of their names. As *tn* it may similarly convey the idea of *distinction into kinds*. Also *Tenu* was the name of an important tribe on the N.E. of Egypt, in Palestine; *Methen* is perhaps an interpreter (?) or foreign resident (?), an emigrant or immigrant. After O.K., in both the values *qmʾ* and *tn*, is in hieratic generally accompanied by a bird, , to show that it is the throw-stick and not the finger, ; and after the XIXth Dynasty this bird appears regularly in the hieroglyphs in the attitude of one struck by the throw-stick, , &c., as shown in the fowling scenes. is a barbarous form.

[*B. H.*, iii., fig. 23.] Fisherman's boat containing a net, or a fish (*Siut*, Tomb i., l. 248).

Word-sign for *wḥʿ* (*uḥá*), "catch fish and birds," "fisherman"; the word is often spelt phonetically in O. and M.K. (*Pyr.*; *Siut*, *l.c.*; *El B.*, ii., Pl. xvi.). Phon. trans. to many other words.

[*B. H.*, iii., fig. 47.] Paddle.

Name, *ḥp·t*; with rad. ext. as det. Word-sign for *ḫrw* (*kheru*), "voice" (occasionally also *ḫry*, "enemy"), possibly in reference to the cry or song with which time was marked in paddling.

Fig. 112. A harpoon, the head (of bronze (?), coloured green, perhaps originally grey) is barbed and fitted by a tang into the wooden shaft; a loop of cord is tightly lashed on or near the head, for the fixing of the line; in O.K. the barb is always single.

Word-sign for , *wʿ* (*uá*), "one," perhaps in reference to its being single-headed, as opposed to the bident of fishing scenes (L., *D.*, ii., 130—XIIth Dyn.), or because of the single barb, *v.* . But war-darts are perhaps called *wʿ* (*uá*), Düм., *H. I.*, i., Pl. xx.; the first sign, however, is imperfect. The usual name of a harpoon, bident or other, is (*Pyr. P.*, l. 424), *mʿbʾ* (*mába*), which is the name also of the numeral 30, and so is accompanied by . The etymology of the name is unknown.

Fig. 56; *B. H.*, iii., fig. 71. Harpoon-head of white bone or ivory; cf. the "prehistoric" harpoon-heads of bone in Petrie, *Naqada*, Pl. lxi. In M.K. it is sometimes joined with , the string which bound it to the shaft (L., *D.*, ii., 121). In N.K. its origin seems to have been forgotten, and an impossible form is substituted (fig. 56 or) preserving a reminiscence of this string.

In *Pyr. P.*, l. 425, the two points of a bident weapon are called *qś·wi* (*qes·ui*), "the two bones." Thus, as was conjectured in *B. H.*, iii., p. 24, the name of the harpoon-head is *qś*, "the bone." But the sign is not only used as the word-symbol for "bone," and as phon. for *qś*; by a most exceptional procedure this picture of a manufactured article of bone is id. of (A) many kinds of bone-like materials and objects, and (B) apparently of matters connected with the disposal of the bones of the skeleton in the grave.

(A) is det. of "ivory," , *'b* (*ab*); of the names of all reeds—no doubt on account of their polished surface; of *b'* (*bá*), "rib of the palm-leaf," "palm-stick"; and of , *m'w·t* (*mau·t*), "stalk of corn," "shaft of spear," &c.

Note that Heb. קָנֶה *ḳâneh* (which appears in N.K. Egyptian as *qnn*, Lat. *canna*), means "reed," "hollow corn-stalk," "spear-shaft," and "humerus bone," thus almost covering the above significations of .

, *twr* (*tur*), "the clean," as the name of a reed (?), is perhaps the origin of the det. in *twr*, "purify." But see the compound , below, no. 2.

(B) is, from earliest times, det. of the word *qrś*, "funerary equipment," "coffin," probably because of the connexion both in sound and idea with "bone." Erman (*Gram.*) and Max Müller (*Orientalistische Litteratur-zeitung*, 1898, 17) both consider the two words to be radically connected. Also, from *Pyr.* onwards, det. of *gn·t*, "posthumous fame," "memory of the dead."

is the sculptor of statues with mallet and chisel, who also finishes them with paint-pot and brush; see *B. H.*, ii., Pl. iv., right, and Pl. xiii., left; in the similar scene, Ros., *M. C.*, xlvi., 9, which is probably copied from the tomb of Aba, XXVIth Dyn., the word is written . In Ros., *M. C.*, xlv., 5 (also Aba), the makes *ushabtis*; in Ch., *M.*, clxxx. = Ros., *M. C.*, xlvii., 1 (Aba), he sculptures a lion. In the tomb of Min, *temp.* Thothmes III. (*Miss.*, v., 366), the is working on a sacred boat with mallet and chisel.

It is difficult to decide how came to have the meaning of "sculptor." The carving of bone and ivory into harpoon heads, pins and ornaments, was evidently an important art in prehistoric and early Egypt, and though this work would seldom require mallet and chisel, it may have given its name to a more developed technique. Or again, the sacred stone-mason was called "necropolis-man," and in the same way the sculptor of *ka*-statues, *ushabtis*, and other burial equipment may have been called "skeleton-" or "bone man," or "burial-man," since his work was chiefly for the tomb.

From very late variants quoted in the dictionaries, it would seem that this ancient word (, *Ptahhetep*, Pl. xxxii.) must be read *msn·ti*, not *gn·ti*, which would otherwise appear a probable reading as denoting "preserver of the *gn·t*, i.e. the memory of the dead."

occurs in the compound signs (1) , *sḥ*, "toe" (Lange, *Ä. Z.*, 1896, p. 77), in which , the bone, is sometimes in very early cases replaced by , the finger; but the origin of the sign is not yet perfectly clear. (2) , *bd*, "natron," in which the species of indicating toilet powders seems to be defined as that used for funerary purposes, , or in particular, perhaps for the washing of the bones, . It can hardly be doubted that the bone-sign acquired a det. meaning in connexion with funeral rites; "thy bones are purified" is a common expression in the funeral ritual, and mummification was not a very early invention in Egypt, being little practised even at the end of the O.K. (On this subject see Petrie, *Deshasheh*, p. 15 *et seqq.*).

[*B. H.*, iii., fig. 42, wrongly in the plate.] Straight bar ending in a double hook: possibly a fish-hook of bronze, coloured red.

Word-sign for *rtḥ*, "bind," "tame," and *ḫn*[*r*] (*khen*[*er*]), "prison," &c., with phon. trans. in each value. *ḫnt* and appear to be confused with it in the second value *ḫn*, *ḫnr*, owing to their identical forms in hieratic (see *Kah. Pap.*, i., l. 8).

Fig. 52. Bird-trap consisting of two curved frames (the nets filling these frames are sometimes also shown). For the hieroglyph, cf. *Medum*, x., xviii.; and *B. H.*, ii., Pls. vi., xiv., for various forms of bird-traps.

The name of the net-trap is *ybt* (*ȧbt*). The sign is also word-symbol for *śḫt* (*śekhet*), "catch with a net or trap," also "weave," "plait," "construct of reeds," &c.

N. Furniture, Food, Personal Accoutrements, Writing, Music, Games.

Fig. 65. Portable chair, somewhat as figured in *Medum*, Pl. xxi.; *El B.*, i., Pl. xiii., &c.

This sign is found among dets. of (*y*)*s·t* (*ȧs·t*), "throne," in *Pyr.*; *W.*, ll. 391, 393. It is also det. of other words of similar meaning, e.g. *wṯs* (*uthes*), *ḫnd* (*khend*), *ṯ'n·t* (*than·t*).

In N.K. the name of Osiris, usually *ys-yr* (*ȧs-ȧr*), was regularly written, the being replaced by, probably because of the more ceremonial significance of the latter sign.

[*B. H.*, iii., fig. 86.] Conventionalized throne. The form is very unpractical for a seat, but perhaps it is intended for the throne of a statue. The colour varies: in L., *D.*, ii., 21, it is yellow, for wood; in *Medum*, Pl. xiii., it is white, for limestone; here we have blue, for dark stone.

The reading of the name as *ś·t* alone is probably wrong. It should in all likelihood be *yś·t* (*ȧs·t*), with weak initial (omitted in writing). As phon., seems normally to represent, and after O.K., but the —soon reduced to —was sometimes neglected in early writing. In *Pyr.* is a variant for, and the latter is sometimes alph. for *ś*.

As to the group for the name of Osiris, Erman (*Gram.*) is inclined to render the name *Wś·yr* (*Uś·ȧr*), and he gives to ordinarily the value of *ś* alone. But *Yś·yr* rather than *Ś·yr* would be the closer rendering of *Wś·yr*. As the group had the appearance of meaning "throne of the Eye," *yś·t yr·t* (*ȧs·t ȧr·t*), the throne was generally placed below the eye.

Word-sign for *ḥtm*, meaning "destroy," "complete," &c. The origin of this value is unknown.

Fig. 136; *B. H.*, iii., fig. 66. Box or casket of variable form, with or without feet and arched cover; especially representing a coffin.

Named *hn*. Det. of its own name, which is applied to boxes of any shape or size, casket or coffin. In the form, det. of coffins and burial.

Fig. 126; *B. H.*, iii., fig. 21. Stand for food and drink: naturally very variable.

(1) In fig. 126 it has the form of a rack for jars of liquid—water, beer, or wine—containing two water coolers (*ḥes·t*), and one short covered vessel (*nemś·t*); in the lower part of the rack is a shelf upon which the bases of the two tall vessels rest. See Maspero, *Trois années*, Pl. ii., for a similar stand with names to the vases.

(2) Another form is, for combined food and drink.

(3) Or again, it may be, the bread-stand, so constantly figured in the scene of the "table of offerings." This represents a table covered, not with a garnishing of leaves, as has been suggested (*Ä. Z.*, 1893, p. 1) and agreed to by many, but with halves, quarters, or at any rate slices of tall pointed loaves of bread, laid parallel; see *Medum*, Pl. xiii., where both in form and colour the slices are precisely halves of the in the accompanying inscription; so also on the panels of Hesy. Later figures are less definite, and in the M.K. the slices are often represented so conventionally as to have become almost meaningless to the eye.

(1) is word-sign for *wdḥ* (*udh*), "drink-stand." (3) is word-sign for *ḫ'w·t* (*khau·t*), "food-stand." (2) will serve as word-sign for either; in *B. H.*, i., Pl. xvii., it is picture det. of *wdḥ*, of *ḫ'w·t*, and of *ḥtp wsḫ·t*, "offering in the court."

Cf. **Fig. 94**; *B. H.*, iii., fig. 21. Cake of bread, the lower part represented as shaped or marked by the vessel in which it was baked or moulded. In O.K. generally coloured black (*Medum*, in offerings), perhaps because of the crust being burnt; later, often yellow.

Name, *t*, cf. = , *Pyr. W.*, 161, so also , *N.*, 426, &c., commonly in tables of offerings; or perhaps *yt* (*ȧt*); compare its homophony with in (N.K.) and *v.* . The group *tw*, *ytw* (*tu*, *ȧtu*) must not be confounded in value with *t'* (*ta*).

Figs. 17, 62, 179. Short stick with knob at the end, having the appearance of a club, but perhaps only an abbreviated form of the walking-stick, the top of which is formed like the lower end of in its typical form. In the tomb of Tehutihetep (fig. 179) the sign is less symmetrical than usual.

Word-sign for *md*, "walking-stick," "stick," "wand" (Max Müller, *Rec. de Trav.*, ix., 21; *Ä. Z.*, 1893, 126). Used with phon. trans.

Fig. 171; *B. H.*, iii., fig. 18. Scribe's outfit, consisting of palette, pen or pen-case, and water-pot (see *B. H.*, iii., p. 12). According to Borchardt the sculpture on the panels of Hesy (Mar., *Alb.*, Pl. xii.) rather indicates a leather pouch containing dry colour in place of the water-pot; but this is not clear.

Word-sign for the following:

(1) *sš* (*sesh*), "write," believed to be the usual value. , "scribe," is probably to be read *sšw* (*seshu*).

(2) *ṯmś* (*themś*) = "wooden panel," "sculptured or painted (?) designs." Used also by phon. trans.

(3) (*Pyr.*) *ṯrw·t* (*theru·t*), "ink"; later, , *trw*, *wtrw*, "colours for writing and painting." In this word the sign is more det. than word-sign.

(4) *n*ʿʿ (*nȧȧ*), "to be polished"—of stone or wood—"to be smooth," perhaps as a surface for painting; or, more likely, "to be ground fine" like a pigment for writing-ink, or for painting. In medical papyri we have standing also for the causative *ś·n*ʿʿ (*ś·nȧȧ*), "grind fine" (*Kah. Pap.*, p. 8).

The supposed value ʿ*n* (*ȧn*) is entirely wrong; it is due to a misreading of the title *sšw*(?) ʿ *n śtn*, "scribe of the account ( ) of the king."

Figs. 44, 153; *B. H.*, iii., fig. 61. Papyrus rolled up, tied and sealed; by exception there is no seal in fig. 44.

(1) The group (L., *D.*, iii., 148*a*, &c.) appears to be identical with the word written in *Pyr.*, and *š*ʿ·*t* (*shȧ·t*), with various other forms of det. indicating a bundle of papyri. It means a book or writing of any sort, and probably refers to the slicing, *š*ʿ, of the papyrus-pith; cf. .

(2) is also in O.K. to be read ʿ (*ȧ*), as the name of a papyrus or writing, especially of an account or register; cf. (*Methen*, L., *D.*, ii., 3, top), and the ancient title (Mar., *Mast.*, 406) = (*Methen*, L., *D.*, ii., 7*b*) = (panel of Hesy, Mar., *Alb.*, Pl. xii.). Except in titles this word does not seem to occur after O.K. In *Pyr.*, e.g. *T.*, l. 242, "hand" is actually written by an extraordinary transference.

 [*B. H.*, iii., fig. 37.] Flute (?). At Medum, and in other very early instances, generally represented as a narrow rectangle; but in *Ptahhetep*, Pl. xxxiii., it tapers from end to end; later, it has straight sides with a sharp bevel at one end, as in the example figured.

Word-sign for 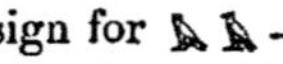 *m^{x}* (*maȧ*), "straight," "just," "true"; an idea that may be connected either with the cubit rod or with the flute. Maspero, Loret, Erman (*Gram.*) all agree that it represents a flute. Loret discussed the question in his *Flutes Égyptiennes Antiques*, pp. 11-13 (*Journal Asiatique*, 1890). , , or its variants, seems to be det. of a word  *m·t*,  *m'·t* (*ma·t*), "oblique flute," and of  *sb*, a "flute," or "to play the flute." Borchardt believes that in early times was a double flute, quoting in confirmation of his theory a scene in the Cairo Museum, and that later perhaps it was a single one. In several O.K. sculptures the flute, held obliquely, is named 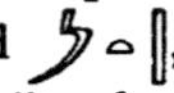,  *m'·t* (*ma·t*), a "stick," "cane," and , the straight flute, is 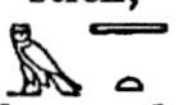 (L., *D.*, ii., 52), which may possibly be read *m^{x}·t* (*maȧt*), though L., *D.*, ii., 74*c*, indicates *m·t* as the reading.

 **Fig. 144.** Draught-board, set with men. The board in plan, divided into three rows of ten squares each; the draughtsmen appearing on the edge, in elevation, are of two sorts; their number varies in different examples.

The draught-board is called 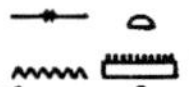 *sn·t*, the game 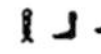 *ḥbᶜ* (*hebȧ*), but the value of this very common phon. is 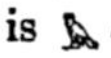 *mn*. The root *mn* means especially "firm," "established," and perhaps for this reason the sign is found above false doors in tombs. The draught-board "set" with men and firmly placed seems thus to have symbolized the idea of firmness, and probably was described as ,  *mn*, "set."

O. Insignia, Sceptres, Symbols, Standards.

 **Fig. 22.** The crowns of Upper and Lower Egypt placed side by side, or one within the other, in a *neb*-basket, 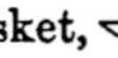. Royal emblems were perhaps carried in such baskets to prevent their contact with profane things.

Word-sign for 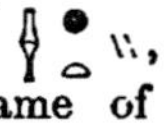,  *sḫm·ti* (*sekhem·ti*), the name of the double crown, lit. "the two powerful (things)."

Det. of 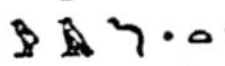 *w'z·ti* (*uaz·ti*), "the two flourishing (things)," and of 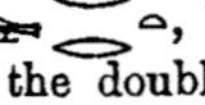,  *wrr·t* (*urer·t*), also names for the double crown. *Wrr·t* is perhaps a form of *wr·t*, "the great," strengthened by reduplication of the final radical.

 Cf. **Fig. 22.** White crown of Upper Egypt, consisting of a tall cap, perhaps made of silver (or of white cloth).

Name, 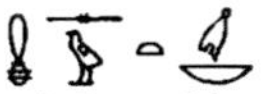 *mys·wt* (*mȧs·ut*); also 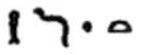 *ḥz·t*, "the white."

 Cf. **Fig. 22.** Red crown of Lower Egypt, consisting of a cap or circlet, perhaps always open at the top, as when the upper crown is fitted into it. At the middle of the back rises a bar sloping slightly backwards, and from the inside a coil  projects upwards and forwards. Perhaps the red crown was made of copper.

Name,  *N·t*, also *dšr·t* (*desher·t*), "the red." The former name gave rise to the alph. value *n*, traceable in M.K. and common in N.K. Often also the sign is equivalent to , as word-symbol for *by·ti*, "king of Lower Egypt," for which value see Sethe, *Ä. Z.*, 1890, p. 125; 1892, p 113.

 [*B. H.*, iii., fig. 52.] Coil; the form is that of the coil in , and the colouring—black—is that often used in representing symbols (cf. , ).

Word-sign for *šn·t* (*shen·t*) (*B. H.*, i., Pl. xxx., corresponding to the true rope  in

Tehutihetep, *El B.*, i., Pl. xxvii., l. 11), occurring in a title, for which see *Kah. Pap.*, p. 26; Moret, *Rec. de Tr.*, xvii., 44, and which may possibly refer to examination by torture, or to binding. The coil on the crown is named  *ḥʾb* (c̲hab), "coil." Its use in this title indicates that on the royal crown it symbolizes authority to bind, &c. In this connexion we may also note the symbolism of the rope in the word 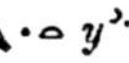 *yʾ·t* (*àa·t*), "official rank" (from kingly to that of lowest officer), of which it is det. in *Medum*, Pl. xx. (, initial being omitted). Compare the word-sign , for *yʾ·t*, with variant forms, e.g. L., *D.*, ii., 97*b*.

 Fig. 39. Crook sceptre, coloured yellow (?), and in all detailed pictures with joints like a cane, but probably of wood with metal plating. In the early examples (*Medum*, Pls. x., xxviii., 6; and *Methen*), the curve is slight, not turning downwards, . Cf. the remarkable banded sceptre, very slightly curved, in the hand of the Aam Sheikh, *B. H.*, i., Pl. xxviii. Later it assumed the form of our present example (cf. *B. H.*, i., Pl. xxviii.), probably from confusion with the true shepherd's crook,  (*Methen*, L., D., ii., 5, right side), from which it is derived.

The sceptre , like the shepherd's crook, was named  *ʿw·t* (*àu·t*) (*Pyr.* and M.K. coffins, &c.). This is also the name for flocks and herds, especially of goats, for which the crook and its variant forms are word-sign. The sceptre  is word-sign for 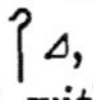,  *ḥq*,  *ḥqʾ* (*ḥeqa*), "king," "ruler," with rad. ext. Once (*Ä. T.*, 37) this name seems to be applied to the sceptre itself. The reading of 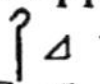 is shown approximately by its use for  in the late text, *Piankhy*, l. 9, &c. There seems also to be a rare value  *yʾq* (*yaq*), *Pyr. W.*, ll. 211, 283, &c.

 Cf. Fig. 148. Emblematic scourge, or fly-flap, jewelled. Held by king, by Osiris as king, and by the god Min.

Name, 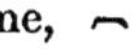 *nḫḫ* (*nek̲hek̲h*), with variants (*Mentuhotep*, p. 19, no. 19). Symbolic of driving away evil; cf. its use in ,  *ḫw* (*k̲hu*), "protect."

 Fig. 104, cf. Fig. 165; *B. H.*, iii., fig. 44, cf. fig. 43. Mallet-symbol, coloured black; later, blue. In fig. 165, however, it seems to be of fine grained wood. The form is nearly that of the light mallets of red wood used by sculptors and flax beaters, and by boat-makers (see Ros., *M. C.*, *passim*). But more especially—as pointed out by Piehl—is it the form of the mallet 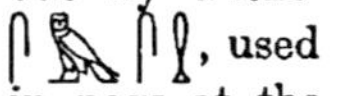, used by kings and deities for driving in pegs at the foundation of a temple, e.g. *Ab.*, i., l., col. 13. It is not found as an actual sceptre.

Word-sign for 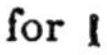 *ḥn*, "servant" (fem. *ḥn·t*, "maid-servant"); connected with the root *ḥn*, "command." It is used, however, in a special and opposite sense, 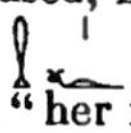 *ḥn·f*, meaning "his majesty," and *ḥn·t·s*, "her majesty" (obelisk of Queen Hatshepsut, &c.), in reference to king, queen, god, and goddess. (Cf. *ḥn·t*, "mistress.") 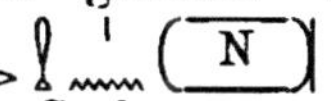 is "during the reign of ...." Such ceremonial expressions may not be very intelligibly constructed; possibly  is in these cases really the sceptre of "authority."

The reading of the word-sign as  *ḥn* seems best shown by  *ḥn* in L., *D.*, ii., 8.

 Figs. 84, 110. *Sekhem* sceptre (banded with green and white). In tomb sculptures this sceptre is constantly seen in the hands of nobles when out of doors but not occupied. Original examples in bronze and wood have the broad end of flattened oval section.

The sceptre ,  (*Ä. T.*, Pl. 38) is frequently mentioned. It is word-sign for 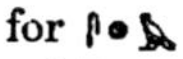 *šḫm* (*śek̲hem*), "powerful," often written ,

N.K. ; the fem. is usually written *śḫm·t*. In *Mentuhotep*, Pl. iii., we have a sceptre of the *sekhem* form called *ʿbʾ* (*ȧba*), which is also word-sign for *ʿbʾ*. This probably means "adornment," see MAX MÜLLER, *Rec. de Tr.*, ix. 169. The word *ḫrp* (*kherp*), "to be commander of," "direct," is usually written —det., arm holding the *sekhem*. But in titles of functionaries seems generally to be read *ḫrp*, from the earliest times. (Cf. = *ḫrp k'ʾt* (*kherp kat*), "director of works").

On the analogy of the last, the type of this sceptre may be developed from a large heavy-headed mallet by flattening the head for lightness. *ḫrp* in *Todt.*, cap. 99, is the name of the heavy mallet which drives the mooring-post, and this mallet is of the same form as that used by quarrymen, &c. It would at least be quite appropriate as an emblem of "power over" a thing (*śḫm*). In *Pyr. P.*, l. 409, &c., there is another instrument , which may be the origin of the sceptre. Both *sekhem* and *aba* sceptres are named in *Pyr.*, but apparently there is no mention of a sceptre named *kherp*.

Fig. 138; *B. H.*, iii., fig. 36. Cylinder seal (?), with string for suspension; or badge of office in imitation of a cylinder seal, . Besides we have , and a form between these two, all three forms being found in *El B.*, i., Pl. xx. The string is usually of beads, perhaps invariably so in O.K. detailed hieroglyphs (*Medum*, front., fig. 12). BORCHARDT, *Ä. Z.*, 1897, p. 106, publishes a fine example of the form from a Vth Dyn. false door from Saqqareh, and shows the possibility of the projection at the lower end being a handle to a metal (?) frame in which a cylinder seal revolves. Professor Petrie had already conjectured that the sign represented a cylinder seal (*Medum*, pp. 32-33). The use of cylinders for seals in the earliest times is now well ascertained (see DE MORGAN, *Recherches*, ii., 235, &c.).

Word-sign for a title, "chancellor" or "high treasurer," and for a word meaning "treasures," &c. The reading is still uncertain, see CRUM, *Ä. Z.*, 1894, p. 65-66.

It would be of great importance to ascertain from facsimiles the precise relation of this = to the *ḫtm* (*khetem*) or "seal," and to the which was hung round the neck of the goat in , *sʿḥ* (*sȧḥ*). It is probable that the first and last are necklaces denoting rank, and imitating the true seal *ḫtm*. In L., *D.*, ii., 96, , in the group "seal" (*Halbpfeiler B.*), differs in shape and colouring from = (both in *Ostseite*).

Cf. Figs. 168, 175; *B. H.*, iii., frontispiece. Hawk-perch, with two ornamental straight plumes at the back; at the end of the horizontal bar a peg passed through it, holding the food trough. A perch is far more appropriate to a hawk than to most of the sacred birds, as e.g. ibis, goose, &c., and is a common det. of divinity (*v.* and). The perch would be distinctive of the sacred hawks kept in the temple as opposed to wild hawks; hence it was used by transference at a very early period as the distinctive support of sacred emblems, whether animate (birds, quadrupeds, parts of animals—e.g.), or inanimate. It is perhaps most commonly seen with the symbols of the nomes.

Its name as "perch of the gods" is *yʾ·t* (*ȧa·t*).

Fig. 187. Symbolic staff with canine head; coloured blue, probably for earlier black. It is remarkable that does not appear among the numerous symbolic staves figured in M.K. coffins.

Word-sign for *wśr·t* (*user·t*) in *Pyr.*;

with rad. ext. The nature of the quality denoted by this word may be learnt from the fact that it is distinct from  "authority," "power," as exercised upon a person or thing; it seems rather to denote canine powers of free, swift movement, intelligence. Note also the common formula 

"*ákh* in heaven before Ra, *user* on earth before Geb, *maá-kheru* (triumphantly appealing for blessedness) in the underworld before Osiris." Thus the canine *user* seems to represent earthly resource, power and wealth, just as the winged *ákh* stands for heavenly power.

[In *Sign Pap.*, p. xviii., l. 3,  is explained by the word  *wśr·t*, confirming Lauth's conjecture that *wśr* must be the Coptic ⲃⲁϣⲟⲣ (fem.), which according to the evidence of Hesychius *ap.* Peyron was a *Libyan* name for the fox.]

 [Cf. *B. H.*, iii., fig. 67.] A kind of sceptre with canine head, the ears long and laid back.

The name of this sceptre is  *w'ś* (*uaś*), or fem. *w'ś·t*; with phon. trans. A similar sceptre with twisted handle is named  *z'm* (*zám*). Such sceptres are commonly seen in the hands of the gods. The name of the Oxyrhynchite nome, 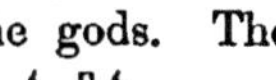 = 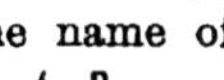 (*Pyr.* variants of *M.*, l. 182), seems to be *W'bw·t*, 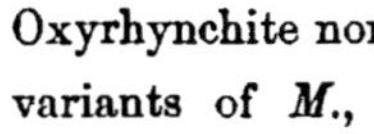 (L., *D.*, ii., 149, *d*), which gives another value, *w'b*, for , probably due to local mythology.

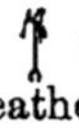 [*B. H.*, iii., fig. 67.] The *uas*-sceptre with feather. The forms in *Pyr.* are very curious, showing an ostrich feather on a staff, which is apparently twisted with a very strong spiral twist, and forked below.

As a name of Thebes, 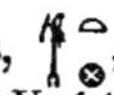, this is supposed to read 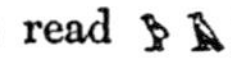 *W'ś·t* (*Uaś·t*). It appears in the name of one of the offerings, probably with the same meaning, and is sometimes placed on the  like the symbol of the Theban nomes. The only important variant for this is  *yt nr* (or *m·t*), "vulture's perch (?)," *Pyr. T.*, l. 76 (cf. the worship of Mut at Thebes); but this is probably not the reading of the sign.

 Fig. 13. Scorpion, much conventionalized, holding in each of its pincers a small abbreviated  "life," and joined by a band to the ring, Ω, "million," *q.v.* (From *D. el B.*, i., Pl. xi.; cf. also *l.c.*, ii., Pls. xxxiii., xlv.).

The scorpion, 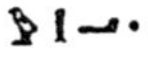 *wḥ'·t*, here no doubt represents the goddess *Śrq·t*, or 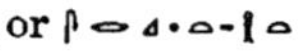 *Śrq·t ḥt*, "the piercer," or "the piercer of the throat"—i.e. to admit air. This goddess is in fact sometimes represented by  in late texts (cf. Birch, *Ä. Z.*, 1870, p. 19). She was one of the vivifying and protecting goddesses, and the present composite symbol—which is placed amongst others denoting divine blessings near the figure of the king in certain religious scenes—may indicate renewing the power of respiration for millions of times.

The sign is not used in ordinary inscriptions.

 Fig. 14. A *ded*-pillar, , with uplifted human arms supporting  (*q.v.*, p. 32). This symbol is used in the same connexion as the last (cf. *D. el B.*, ii., Pl. xxxiii.).

The  was emblematic of stability. The arms may represent the  *ka*, and are often added to emblems. The  also seems to mean "firm."

The symbol therefore apparently signifies "firm," "stable."

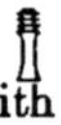 Cf. Fig. 14. Symbolic pillar, properly with tenon at top (*Medum*, Pl. xiii.). In *Todt.*, cap. 155, it is symbolical of the backbone of Osiris. Petrie, *Medum*, p. 31, has suggested that it represents a row of four pillars, the

capitals appearing as though one above, i.e. beyond, another. More probably the symbol is conventionalized from a sacred tree with branches lopped and forming the pillar of a house; cf. the story in PLUTARCH, *De Is.*, cap. 15.

Name, 𓊽𓂧 *zd*, "the firm," with rad. ext. Amulet for stability.

𓊽 **Fig. 24.** An object not unlike four bowls of different colours, nested together and having a small rounded projection at the top. The colours are probably conventional. It closely resembles the top of the 𓊽.

Word-sign for 𓈙𓂝 *š*ʿ (*shā*), "cut," with phon. trans., perhaps referring to the lopping of the branches for the 𓊽. Later the word became 𓈙𓂝𓂧 *š*ʿ*d* (*shād*) (cf. *m*ʿ*r* = *m*ʿ*rd*, s.v. 𓌻), and this is found in a late text as the name of the upper part of the 𓊽 (BR., *Wtb.*, 134*b*). But perhaps owing to its connexion with the *ded* representing the backbone of Osiris, 𓊽 is connected also with the vertebrae or joints, called 𓄦 of the backbone, and so may be det. of "back." We may therefore prefer to associate its value with the division—as it were the "slicing" of the backbone into vertebrae—and to consider it as representing four articulated vertebrae.

𓋹 **Fig. 135.** In the earliest examples the symbol of life is coloured black (*Medum*, Pl. xiv. and p. 33), often with arms and upright drawn as though each were divided longitudinally. Professors Sayce and Petrie saw in it the fisherman's girdle (*Medum*, *l.c.*). In any case the sign probably represented a knot or tie of some kind, perhaps amuletic. On M.K. coffins the 𓋹 is painted blue or green (STEINDORFF, *Mentuhotep*, p. 20, Pl. iv.), and is placed at the foot-end with the sandals; this again suggests that it is a girdle. It may be that it was attached as symbolical of life to a victim or reprieved prisoner.

The sign has the value 𓂝𓈖𓐍 ʿ*nḫ* (*ānkh*), with many meanings, chief of which is "life," of which 𓋹 is the well-known symbol.

𓌀 [*B. H.*, iii, fig. 39.] Ceremonial forked object, used in the ritual of the dead.

Its name has two forms, 𓎡𓆑 𓊪𓋴𓈙 *kf pšš* (*kef pešesh*) and *pšš kf*, which may mean respectively "divider of the united," and "uniter of the divided"; but cf. MASPERO, *Table d'Offrandes*, p. 12; PIEHL, *Sphinx*, ii., p. 34. Borchardt would derive the symbol from a well-known form of ornament, cf. *Mentuhotep*, Pl. iv., and p. 24 (no. 57); but the reference to BR., *Wtb.*, p. 1269, seems to afford no support for this theory, as it gives only part of the usual list of offerings. It may possibly be connected with 𓄿, the bicornate uterus of animals, which perhaps is symbolized in the two feathers 𓋚 of the nome of Eileithyia, and is associated with ram's horns in the head-dresses of gods of generation. Cf. also *Ab.*, i., p. 78, for Osiris Anzti wearing 𓌀 instead of 𓋚, if this is not a mistake of the sculptor.

𓋀 [*B. H.*, iii., fig. 25.] Standard of the West. Ostrich feather on an object resembling the hieroglyph 𓏏, through which is a string or thread, 𓋴. In O.K. the type is with the hawk added, 𓋁. As Maspero has pointed out, the earliest form of the symbol of the West is seen in a schist plaque in the Louvre (*Rev. Arch.*, 1890, Pl. iv.), where a man carries a staff surmounted by a hawk and ostrich feather, arranged much as in 𓋁, and with two straight plumes hanging obliquely behind, somewhat like those attached to the 𓋉 in *B. H.*, iii., frontispiece.

Word-sign for 𓇋𓋀𓈖𓏏𓆇 *Ymn·t* (*Āment*), "the West," with rad. ext. to other forms of the root, e.g. 𓇋𓏠𓈖 *ymn*, "right-hand" = ימן *ymn*, "right-hand." This value changed very early to 𓃹𓅓 *wnm* (*unem*) for "right-hand," which word was probably only a form of the last produced by metathesis; it even varies with *ymn* in *Pyr.* (cf. ERMAN, *Ä. Z.*, 1893, 82). For "West" the original value was retained, and after O.K. *wnm* was generally written .

It may here be remarked that in the sign the is perhaps phonetic, indicating the fem. ending of the name "West." The idea of "the West" is symbolized by the ostrich feather, ostriches being then abundant throughout the Libyan desert. The symbolism of the hawk is not very clear, but the cord , sometimes appearing like a piece of cloth, may be connected with the arts of spinning and weaving, cf. , , which were held in high estimation by the Libyans.

[*B. H.*, iii., fig. 26.] Standard of the East. The form at Beni Hasan, *l.c.*, , with two plumes between two pellets, is confirmed by *El B.*, i., Pl. xv., bottom row, to right. The usual form is ; in the archaic schist plaque of the Louvre the pole ends in a tongue-like object between two small (?); the cross-bar below is broad and rounded, and the two straight plumes hang at the back; but the work is too rough to fix the details.

Word-sign for *y'b't* (*aab't*), "the East," "left-hand," &c.; with phon. transf.

The two balls may be explained as of incense from the South-East, Punt, &c. (on the schist plaque replaced by censers). The feathers may be due to a misunderstanding; the earlier and more typical object like a spear-head may be a flame, or more probably a blade-shaped ingot of bronze, such as might have been imported from the North-East. Such a sign , indicates the useful metals in O.K., see L., *D.*, ii., 49*b* (melting metal), and *Medum*, Pl. xiii., left top, where ingots coloured blue and pink show the material of the objects beneath. In *Medum*, Pl. xv., an of *ḥsmn* corresponds to an of blue in Pl. xiii., and *ḥsmn* is coloured blue in the later paintings (cf. LEP., *Die Metalle*, Pl. ii., fig. 4, &c.). In the "sportive" hieroglyphs of *B. H.*, ii., Pl. xiv. (left) = L., *D.*, ii., 143, *a*, the standard of the East would seem to be a spear without the crossbar or pellets.

P. UNCLASSIFIED.

Fig. 158. A sign apparently representing a slender wooden upright, bearing a crosspiece; perhaps occurring only here (*El B.*, i., Pl. xv., lower left).

The group probably stands for , *ḥm'wt* (*ḥem'ut*), "craftsmen." is, in fact, very nearly identical with the hieratic character for , *wb'*, "to bore," and *ḥm't*, "artificer," and may be taken from it. But it may be actually the picture of some kind of boring instrument, with cross-bar instead of a weighted handle as in . For , see BORCHARDT, *Ä. Z.*, 1897, p. 107; MAX MÜLLER, *Rec. de Trav.*, ix., 161-2.

Fig. 67. A bar of wood crossed above the middle by a shorter bar; a cord binding, or wound round, the junction. In the early paintings (cf. *Medum*, Pls. xi., xxvii.), the object is coloured red throughout, and there is no binding. The present form is perhaps a corruption of the earlier . The sign may represent a winder for thread (?). Unfortunately Professor Petrie has not offered any explanation of it in his most suggestive chapter on the hieroglyphs of Medum.

Common word-sign with the value *nz*. In the word , *śnz*, "fear," may be phon., but more probably the word is a pseudo-causative form of (cf. p. 6).

Fig. 81. Two-barbed spear-head (?), coloured red (in XVIIIth Dyn.), and therefore presumably of wood or bronze. In O.K. it has the same form (*Methen*, &c., &c.). The ordinary printed form, [hieroglyph], is barbarous; like certain other types used in printing, it belongs to a base period, and has nothing to do with the real nature of the object represented.

Word-sign for [hieroglyphs] *šn*, the root *šn* meaning the quality of things that go in pairs, that are equal: "two," "duplicate," "pair," "brother," "sister," &c.; and also "breathe," "smell." [hieroglyph] *šn* is the name of the posts or flag-staffs set up before temples, &c.; perhaps in early times they had the form [hieroglyph], with wedge-like base. When one considers that the Arab sheikh sticks a spear upright in the ground before his tent door, it suggests that the [hieroglyph] is a blunt wooden spear or spear-head for ceremonial purposes. It is probable, too, that [hieroglyphs] *sn·t* (*B. H.*, i., Pl. xxxiv., better in L., *D.*, ii., 130) is connected with a spear or spear-head. The value *šn* may be due to the "two" barbs, as opposed to the harpoon *wʿ*, which in O.K. is always represented with "one" barb only.

[hieroglyph] Fig. 115. Piece of wood, rounded below, tapering to a point at the top where it is curved over.

Value, [hieroglyphs] *ty* (*tá*). In N.K. the sign was adopted as homophone of [hieroglyph], where a tall sign was required in grouping hieroglyphs, [hieroglyph] being used as the corresponding long sign. The meaning and name of the sign are alike doubtful.

[hieroglyph] Fig. 102. A curious sign consisting of a white package attached to a curved stick, a red object projecting above and below the package—perhaps the ends of a tie, but the upper one is pointed like a knife.

Word-sign for [hieroglyphs] *šmš* (*shemš*); cf. [hieroglyphs] PIERRET, *Ä. Z.*, 1879, 136; ERMAN, *Ä. Z.*, 1891, 38; *Ab.*, ii., 43 = ROUGÉ, *Inscr. hiérogl.*, 2 (VIth Dyn.), and [hieroglyphs], LEVI, *Voc.* (from *Bul. stel.*, 29247); meaning "servant," "attendant," "follower." More often, however, it is found written [hieroglyphs], as if spelt *šš* (*sheš*).

Det. of the [hieroglyphs], *Pyr.*, *M.*, l. 608; [hieroglyphs], *N.*, l. 1213; [hieroglyphs], *P.*, l. 425, "he who watches the hand" as a retriever, probably the tame cat that accompanied its master on marsh expeditions, to retrieve birds for him (cf. NAV., *Todt.*, ch. xxxix., l. 5). [hieroglyph] is often figured in the sacred barks of the sun and of Sokaris, no doubt representing their attendants.

Presumably the sign pictures the apparatus carried by an attendant for his master, and thus becomes a symbol and id. of attendance.

[hieroglyph] Fig. 51. A staff, angulated near the top and tied round at the angle, resembling the article of dress called [hieroglyphs] *pd ʿḥʿ* (*ped áhá*), which is always represented in pairs, but the use of which is undetermined (cf. *Mentuhotep*, Pl. iii.).

In M. and N.K. word-sign for [hieroglyphs], [hieroglyphs] *rš*, "to be awake," "to have the mind alert," the substantive [hieroglyphs] *rš·wt* meaning a "dream." The object reminds one of the staff and loop held by the figure of the watchman, guard, herdsman [hieroglyph], which is very variable in form. In *Pyr.*, the word *rš* is written with [hieroglyphs] (*W.*, l. 186), the groups being sometimes [hieroglyphs], [hieroglyphs], [hieroglyphs]. Probably in these cases [hieroglyph], a sign of many values, represents a watchman's staff, and is sometimes used in pairs because there would often be two watchmen seated opposite one another at the entrance to a building.

Confused with [hieroglyph], *q.v.*

[hieroglyph] Fig. 77. BORCHARDT, *Ä. Z.*, 1897, 106, figures this hieroglyph as it appears on the beautiful wooden tablets of Hesy (IIIrd Dyn.) (photographed, MAR., *Alb. de Boul.*, Pl. xii.). As he points out, it is nearly identical with the formidable whip of twisted thongs in O.K.

scenes of driving rams over the ground to break it up, "plough it," as it is said in the inscription. Compare the whips, L., *D.*, ii., 106*b*, with the examples of in *Ptahhetep*, Pl. xxxi. The forms of the sign are curious in their varieties, and it requires further investigation.

Word-sign for *mḥ*, "fill," "north," &c. It may be derived from *ḥ*, "strike," with prefixed *m*, or from *mḥ*, "flax," or *mḥ·t*, "diadem."

Phon. for *mḥ*.

Fig. 55. A packet (?), gland (?). Its occasional variation with rather indicates that it is a packet.

This sign is very common in the medical papyri, in the first place as the word-sign for *wt* (*ut*), in the verbal sense of "poultice" (elsewhere "embalm"), and secondly as det. of fat, soft secretions, pustules, &c. It may also stand alone as ab. for *zd'* (*zeda*), "fatted," of animals and birds, for *wẖd·w* (*ukhedu*), "pustules," and for *ḥś*, "dung," and perhaps for some other words; also as det. of strong odour. Anciently the word *ḥśb* "account," "count," was written ×, the det. × indicating "separate classification," "enumeration in separate categories"; after O.K. it is regularly written , , and by phon. trans. becomes the word-sign of several words *ḥsb*. Possibly this may be accounted for by the above value *ḥś* leading to the substitution of for × as det. of *ḥsb*, and on this followed quickly its use as the word-sign for *ḥsb*.

Fig. 140, cf. Fig. 60. An open stand (?), possibly a kind of funnel, drain or sink. Somewhat variable. The colouring and form of base and sides are in the present instance identical with those of in fig. 123, except that the sides of the triangle are truncated and support a red bowl-shaped object which rests on a red cylinder. (In our reproductions, figs. 140 and 123, the greenish-blue base is unfortunately rendered green in one case and blue in the other.) In *Medum*, Pl. xiii., the sides and base are white. In the N.K. form (see in fig. 60) it appears to be a stand containing a broad tube, which is contracted in the middle and opens out above and below. The sign often resembles, at least in outline, the lower part of , represented as in *B. H.*, iii., fig. 48, *D. el B.*, ii., Pl. xxviii.; in this the vase is placed in a wooden stand, a small support sometimes rising in the middle of the stand for the base of the vase to rest on. A similar object, combined with a knife, is seen in the id. of the butcher's block (?), *Pyr. N.*, l. 622, (?), *P.*, l. 87, &c., &c., which is perhaps to be read *nm·t*. Miss Paget's copy of this sign, as it occurs in the Pyramid of Pepy, shows it to be identical in form with the present example of the sign . The bowl looks as if it might be intended to receive refuse or liquid, which would be carried down the central support or drain-pipe (?).

Word-sign for *ẖr* (*kher*); with rad. ext. Its meaning is "lower" as opposed to *ḥr*, "upper," a sense which might be symbolized by the lower part of a vessel in its stand, as also by a "sink" (?).

seems to occur once as phon. in , *Pyr. P.*, l. 339 = , *M.*, l. 641; but this may be a mistake.

Fig. 60. Graphic compound, consisting of and , in the present instance connected with , a desert slope, as a kind of det. The is often omitted, and in O.K. replaces the invariably.

Word-sign for *ẖr·t nṯr* (*kher·t nether*), "that which belongs to a god," i.e. the necropolis, place of the dead—cf. the German "Gottesacker." The sandy slope (cf. , the fertile slope) refers to the situation of ancient burial-places above the reach of the inundation on the sandy edges of the Nile valley or on the sandy *gezîrehs* of the Delta. The name seems to be fem.  not , its derivative being 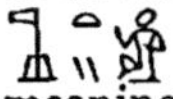 *ḥr'ti ntr*, "man of the necropolis," meaning especially "a mason."

 Figs. 18, 123; *B. H.*, iii., fig. 104. Hollow triangular figure, with small point arising from the centre of the base. In fig. 18 it is coloured green throughout. In the tomb of Merab (L., *D.*, ii., 19) the sign is altogether black; in *B. H.*, iii., fig. 104, the base is blue and the rest black; here, in fig. 123, the base is greenish blue, the point green, and the sides black. At Beni Hasan grey-blue is a frequent colour for representing ground, and black for showing building in brick. In early times black is also the colour for ground; in the XVIIIth Dynasty, green. Hence the colours of our figure may indicate a triangular erection on the ground; but this does not give us the explanation of the sign, which is not without many points of similarity to , fig. 140. 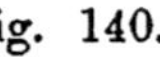 "give," is probably only a graphic compound of word-sign and det., and throws no light on the nature of .

The reading of  is not quite clear. From earliest times 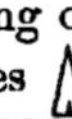 = 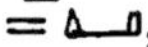,  *d*, or  *dy* (*dā*) (*Pyr. M.*, l. 516 = *P.*, l. 235), and we often find  = 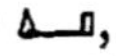, with the meaning "give," "put." STEINDORFF (*Ä. Z.*, 1891, 60) argues that  = , though there is much evidence for reading it as alone. It seems as if *rd*, *dy*, *dd* (?), were all forms of one word, "to give," and that (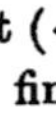)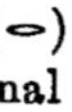(), with fugitive initial *r*, and a weak final *y*, was the root. The question, however, is a delicate one.

The variant  (*Pyr.*, *N.*, l. 33), "humour," "emanation," for  (*Pyr. M.*, l. 195), is apparently a rare case of transference of this word-sign.

 Fig. 36. The sign rather suggests a race-course (Roman *circus*), the green band representing the course itself, the position of the spectators in the middle (*spina*) and the outer horse-shoe stand being coloured blue. But we have no proof that anything of that kind ever existed in Egypt.

Thrice repeated, the sign is placed behind the figure of the king when he is running towards a god (or dancing?) with offerings; usually he is offering the , and the rudder, or two vases of water to Min or Amen (*Koptos*, Pl. ix.; *D. el B.*, i., Pls. xix., xxii.; L., *D.*, iii., 33*g*, *h*, 119*c*, 143*d*). In L., *D.*, iii., 167, the group is omitted; in Ros., *M. C.*, l., 2, a bark is substituted for the rudder as a gift to Nekhebt. In L., *D.*, iii., 57*b*, it occurs where the king is running to Hathor with a crested ibis and symbolical staves. At Abydos the scene does not appear to exist. The sign, still in a group of three, occurs also in the title  (*B. H.*, i., Pl. xxxv.), 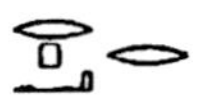  (*Ab.*, ii., 23, l. 7), which possibly denotes the "*erpa* who attends to the  ceremonials in the courtyard."

The reading is unknown.

 Cf. Figs. 9, 178. In some scenes this figure suggests a "rocker" (for a rocking-chair, &c.), Ros., *M. S.*, xl.; MAR., *Ab.*, i., xxii., xxiii., xxxi.*b*. At Deir el Bahri, in the foundation deposits of the temple, a number of small wooden frames were found, perhaps models of rockers, each consisting of two curved boards, , joined together by cross-bars (one, precisely similar, is figured in Ros., *M. C.*, lxvi., 11). They may be connected with the festivals and with the sign .

Det. of names of festivals. After O.K. used as word-sign for  *ḥb*, "festival."

 Fig. 63. Perhaps a case, with open top,

and cord to sling it. Cf. also the panel being painted in *B. H.*, ii., Pl. xiii.; but the resemblance is slight. In *Ab.*, i., Pl. xl.*c*, a 𓎄 is presented to the goddess Sekhemt by the king in the form of a sphinx. 𓎄 may be the case for containing the tools of trade, utensils, &c., and intended to be hung over the shoulder. Cf. the rectangular case often seen by the side or on the back of scribes and attendants in O. and N.K. (L., *D.*, ii., 23, &c.).

Word-sign for 𓎛𓆰𓈖𓎄, 𓎛𓈖 *ḥn* (*ḥen*); very rare in O.K.

In the present instance from *Paheri* (iii. left), 𓎄𓏏𓏥 seems to mean "tasks," or "occupations." Moreover, 𓎛𓆰𓈖𓏌𓅱𓏌𓏥, 𓎛𓈖𓅱 *ḥnw*, constantly has a general meaning of "utensils," "goods."

𓄤 Figs. 49, 164. An object resembling a lute with one peg, or—as in *Medum* and generally in late times—with two pegs. The stem seems graduated for the fingers, and the markings on the belly possibly show the form of the openings in skin stretched over half a gourd. In *Medum*, Pl. xxviii., the colouring of 𓄤 is as in our examples, but in Pls. xxiv., xxvii., the whole object seems to have been coloured red. Mr. Spurrell and Prof. Petrie (*Medum*, p. 30), noting the resemblance of the belly of the instrument with its markings to the heart, suggest that 𓄤 may represent the heart and tracheae. But no anatomical term *nfr* or *nfr·t* is known. The markings are certainly like those on the 𓄣. They may represent the structure of the heart seen in section, and have been transferred to the belly of the lute in the sign 𓄤, where they are constant. Lutes of similar form, but without the markings (?) are figured in the houses of Tell el Amarna (e.g. L., *D.*, iii., 106*a*).

This sign has the phonetic value 𓈖𓆑𓂋 *nfr*, and generally means "good," "beautiful." Br., *Wtb.*, 758, presupposes a name for a lute, "*nfr*" = נבל (*ναῦλα*, *nablium*), and Erman (*Z. D. M. G.*, xlvi., 112) accepts his theory as probable; but this name has not yet been found in Egyptian. *nfr* might mean "adjusted," "tuned," in reference to the lute, since 𓄤𓆑𓂋𓏏𓎛, 𓄤𓆑𓂋𓏏𓌸 *nfr·t*, the "tiller" or "tiller-rope," is probably so called as the "adjuster" of the rudder, and so of the ship.

The absurd inventions which go under the name of the Hieroglyphics of Horapollo, seem to contain a reminiscence of the sign 𓄤. II. 4 runs thus: *Ἀνθρώπου καρδία φάρυγγος ἠρτημένη, ἀγαθοῦ ἀνθρώπου στόμα σημαίνει*, "a man's heart hung from the windpipe means the mouth of a good man." It seems that Horapollo's symbolism treated virtuous speech as a result of direct connexion between the heart and the organs of speech; and it may be that the Egyptians imagined that the windpipe was connected with the heart, and that on this connexion, as figured in 𓄤, depended the goodness, or the health and happiness, of the person.

ADDENDA.

Page ix. (Abbreviations). The opinions cited in this volume under the names of BORCHARDT, LORET, MASPERO, and PIEHL, without specific reference, are those expressed in their respective reviews of *Beni Hasan*, iii., mentioned in the Preface.

Appended are a few necessary corrections. Some of these have been suggested by a study of the valuable squeezes of the tomb of Ptahhetep, lent to the Survey by the authorities of the Berlin Museum, others by the admirable plates of Mr. Newberry's forthcoming edition of the tomb of Rekhmara, proof copies of several having been placed at the disposal of the author.

P. 4, col. 2. An interesting example of the abandonment of flexional consonants is furnished by the word *m·ḥsf*, "spindle," *Todt.*, cap. cliii. (N.K.), giving to the word-sign value *ḥsf* (*khesef*).

P. 16, col. 1. The verb *m* often occurs in O.K., in scenes in which a person shows or offers an object to another to accept. Whether the sign originally signified the *offering* or the *acceptance* (the implied command to accept), it is difficult to decide. The instance in Paheri needs confirmation from earlier sources.

P. 19, col. 1. In *Rekhmara*, Pl. ii., l. 1, occurs apparently with the meaning "a hide," and this probably gives the origin of the value of this sign.

P. 20, col. 2. The Berlin squeezes of Ptahhetep satisfactorily show that the det. of *mnwt* in *Ptahhetep*, Pl. xli., is not , but is more like the pigeons in *l.c.*, Pl. xxxi., &c., with long bill and tail not forked. We must not therefore connect with a pigeon.

P. 27, col. 2. In Syria the threshing-floors are circular, and *edged by large rough stones;* see a figure in HASTINGS, *Dict. of Bible*, i., 50. *ḥw sp·t* occurs also at Zawyet el Maiyitin (L., *D.*, ii., 107, top).

P. 37, col. 2. The spelling of the verb "to eat" in linear hieroglyphs on the coffins of Mentuhotep at Berlin is simply or (the two signs being indistinguishable); *Ä. T.*, Pl. viii., ll. 67, 71, 73. On the coffin of Sebekaa is distinct from , and the verb is written , *Ä. T.*, Pl. xlii., l. 47; , *l.c.*, l. 65; , *l.c.*, Pl. xli., ll. 39-40. The latter coffin, therefore, preserves fully the ancient value, while the former agrees with the usual M.K. spelling .

It is doubtful whether the word for "ulcer" (?) is connected with that for "eating," and the word for "flame" reads *ymyt*, not *wmy·t*. The value *ymi* was thus evidently transferred to other roots than that from which it originated. It is therefore very remarkable that is never used for the simply prepositional or adverbial , and in forms of this root is confined to the adjectival *ymi* and its derivatives *ymitwni*, "between two," &c.

P. 39, col. 1. Some may prefer to connect the name of this with the root *sꜣ*, "guard," rather than with "pass."

P. 44, col. 2. In *El B.*, ii., Pl. v., the plough is drawn by oxen having across their horns as a yoke. Thus is the harness for ox-draught, a bar (in Rekhmara) with cord to fix to pole.

P. 50, col. 2. The reading of the mythological place-name , PETRIE, *Six Temples*, i., 4, is probably *mr dświ*. The sign stands as ab. for *wgś*, "split," in connexion with fish, &c. (add. note to *Kah. Pap.*, xxxix., l. 36).

ERRATA

(To *HIEROGLYPHS* AND *BENI HASAN*, III.).

HIEROGLYPHS.

Pl. viii., figs. 123, 140; the bases should be each of the same colour—greenish blue.

BENI HASAN, III.

Pl. iv., fig. 42.  should be placed horizontally, .

Pl. vi., fig. 89. should be bluish green.

P. 4. Maspero refers to ROUGÉ, *Rev. Arch.*, 1872, tome xxiii., pp. 70-71, for a reading of the Oryx nome-sign as *mḥ·t*. Loret considers the animal to be the *Oryx beisa*, on account of its white colour (cf. the name *m'ḥz*, "the white (?) *m'*"), *leucoryx* being fawn and rust-coloured.

P. 5, fig. 1. For "sixth column from left" read "sixth column from right," as Loret points out.

P. 6, fig. 2. The sign read *wb* by Max Müller is apparently nothing but . The *rḫti* birds, "fullers," are in the best example (L., *D.*, ii., 126 = *B. H.*, I., xxix.) clearly ducks (or geese ?), birds, presumably of white varieties, which splash and preen themselves in the water. But fig. 2 remains a puzzle.

P. 8, fig. 11. A distinguished zoologist has pointed out that it is inaccurate to speak of the "crop" of a duck, the duck tribe being characterized by the absence of the crop.

P. 8, fig. 12. This is to be read *ḥtm*, not 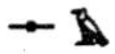; *v.* above, p. 22.

P. 10, note. Professor Maspero notes that M. Joret's paper read before the *Académie des Inscriptions* is published in *Mélanges de Philologie romane dédiés à Carl Wahlund*, pp. 273-80.

P. 22, fig. 36. According to Brugsch the verb  occurs only once, and that in a very late text. It may mean "to cut," but not "to carve," or "to sculpture."

P. 23, note. The reference to PRISSE, *Art Égyptien*, is ii., Pl. 62, according to the arrangement indicated in the Table of Contents.

P. 29, fig. 90. Borchardt considers  to be the armlet often figured on M.K. coffins, with the ties in this case changed to beads.

P. 32, fig. 103. For "to complete" read "to be completed."

ORDER OF THE SIGNS.

A. Humanity.

 pp. 11-13.

B. Anthropomorphic Deities; Human Ranks and Classes.

 pp. 13-14.

C. Human Action.

 pp. 14-16.

D. Mammals and Parts of Mammals.

 pp. 16-19.

E. Birds and their Parts.

 pp. 19-23.

F. Reptiles, Fishes, Insects, &c.

 pp. 23-26.

G. Trees, Herbs, Grasses, &c.

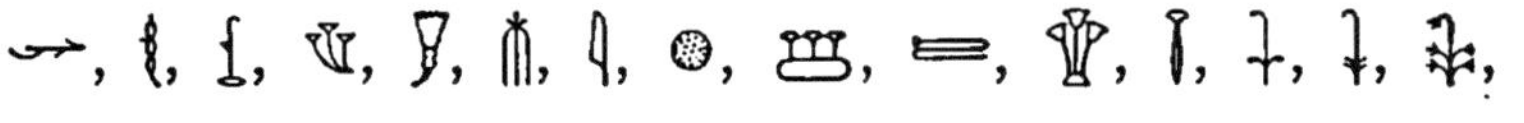 pp. 26-30.

H. Sky, Earth, and Water.

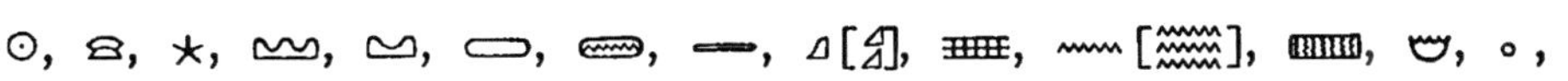 pp. 30-34.

I. Buildings and their Parts.

pp. 34-39.

J. Vases and Pottery, Fire.

 pp. 39-43.

K. Fibre, Textile, Basket-, Mat-, and Leather-Work.

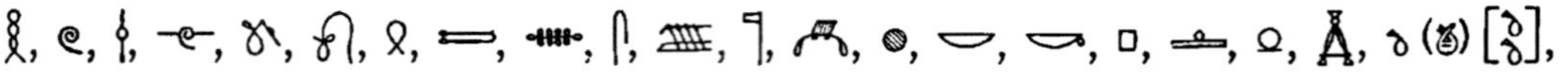
 pp. 43-48.

L. Implements and Tools.

 pp. 48-51.

M. War, Hunting, &c.

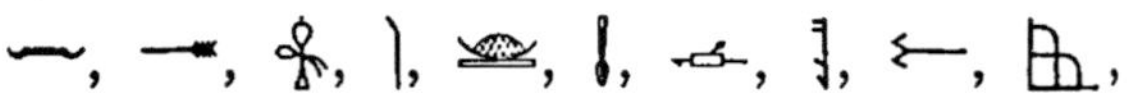 pp. 51-54.

N. Furniture, Food, Personal Accoutrements, Writing, Music, Games.

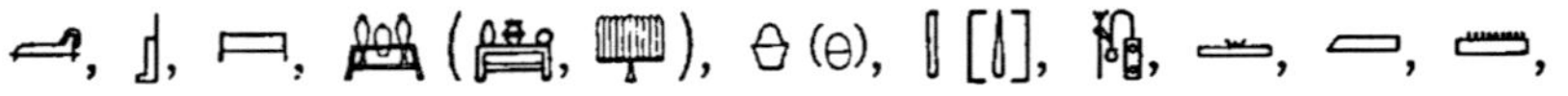 pp. 54-56.

O. Insignia, Sceptres, Symbols, Standards.

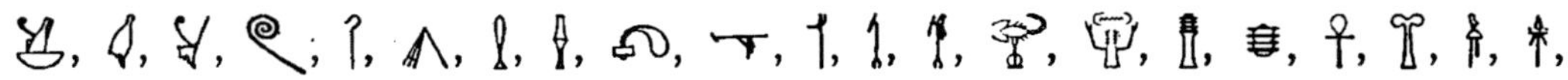
pp. 56-61.

P. Unclassified.

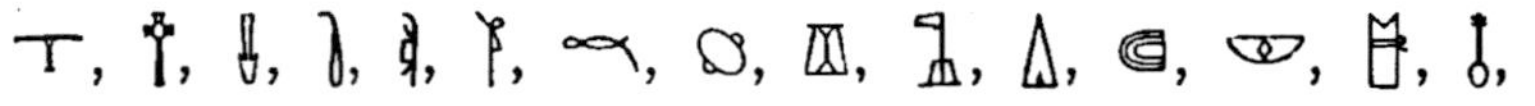 pp. 61-66.

INDEX TO FACSIMILES.

(Including those quoted from *BENI HASAN*, III., and *BENI HASAN*, I.)

BENI HASAN, I.

1

2

3

4

5

Scale--No. 1, full size.
Nos. 2-5, ⅓.

R.F.E.P.

Scale ⅔. DEIR EL BAHRI. *R.F.E.P.*

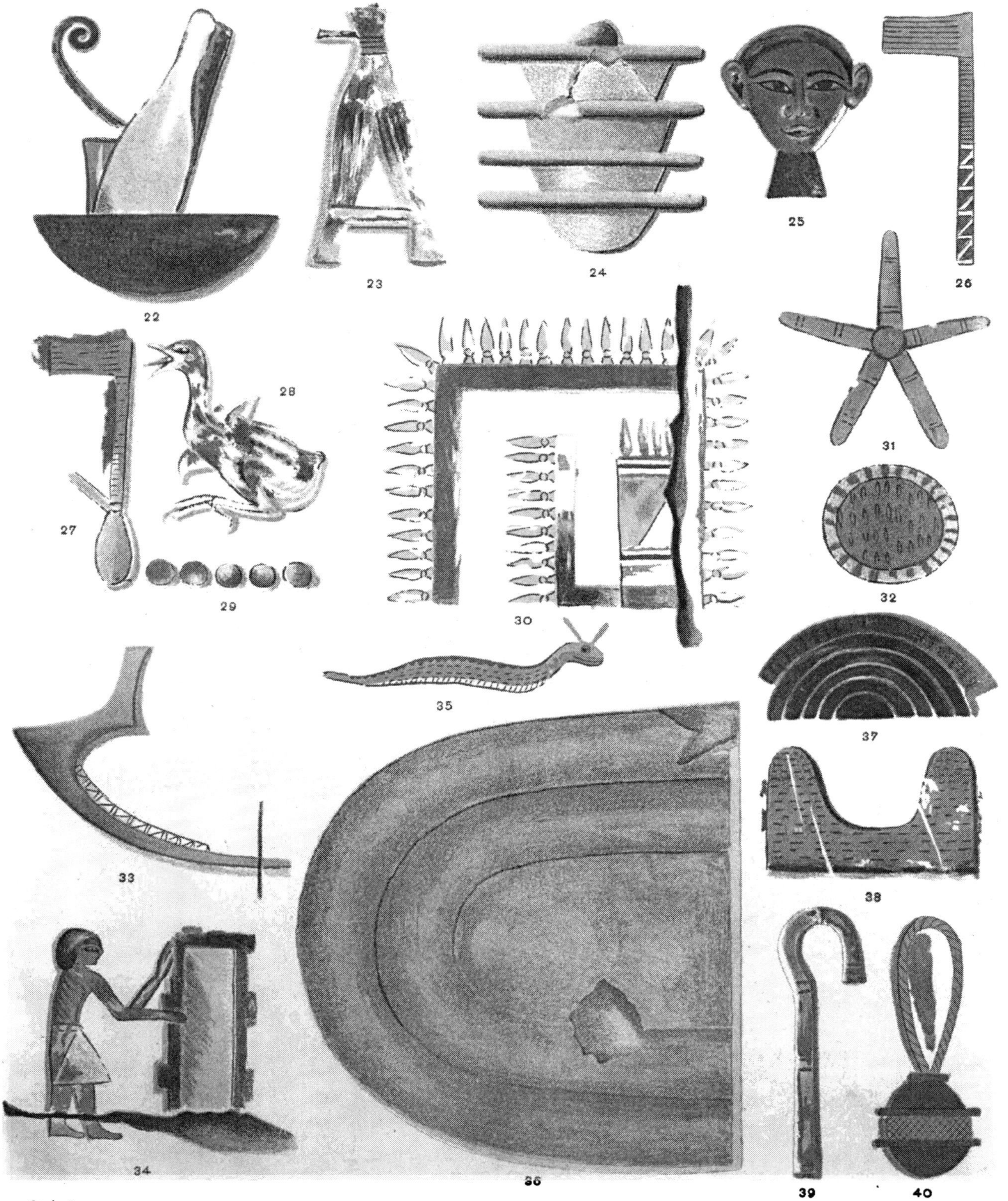
22
23
24
25
26
27
28
29
30
31
32
33
34
35
36
37
38
39
40

41

42

43

44

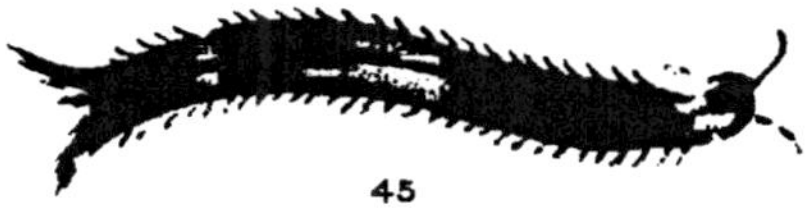

45

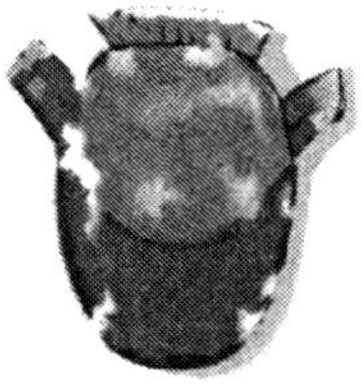

46

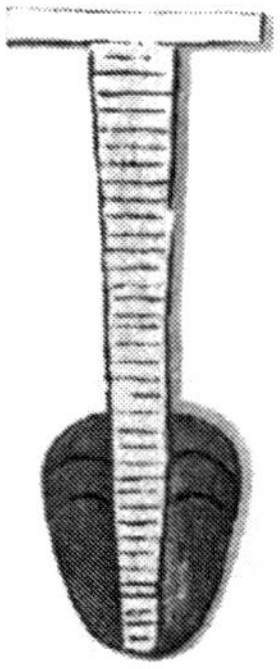

47

48

49

50

51

52

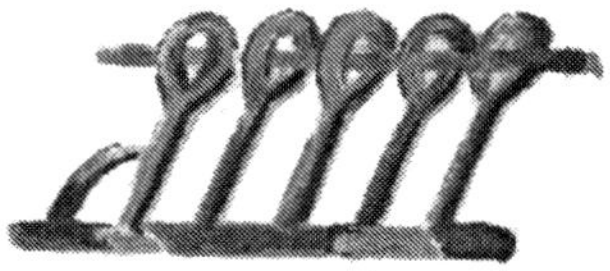

53

54

55

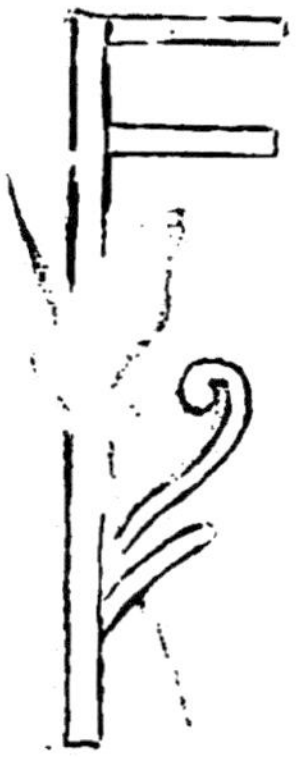

56

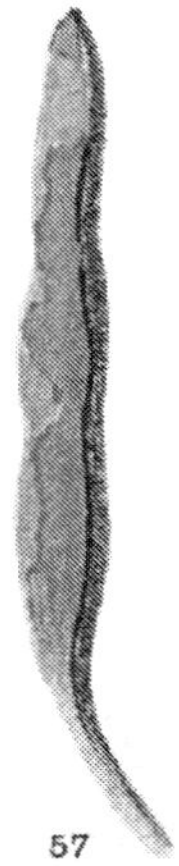

57

60

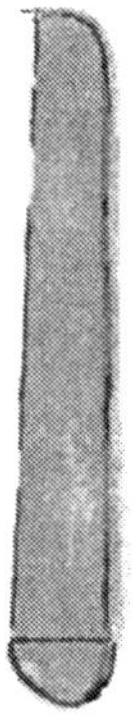

62

63

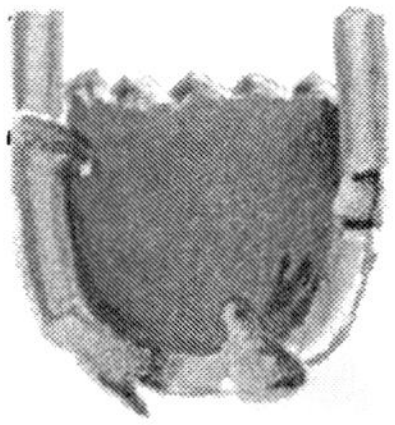

58

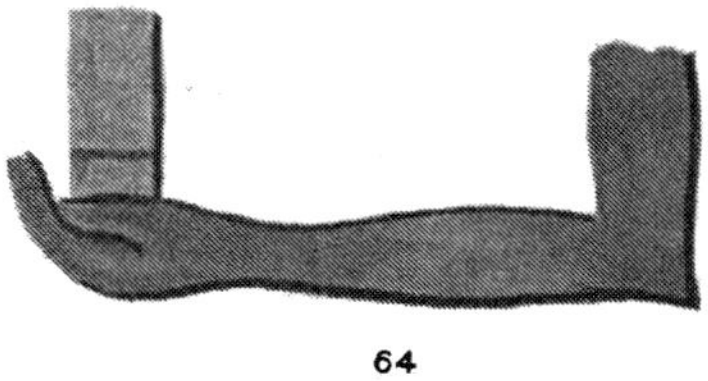

64

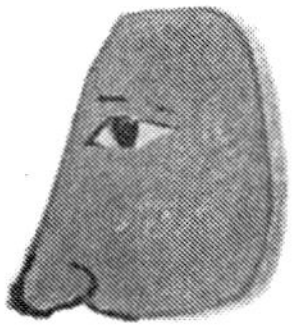

59

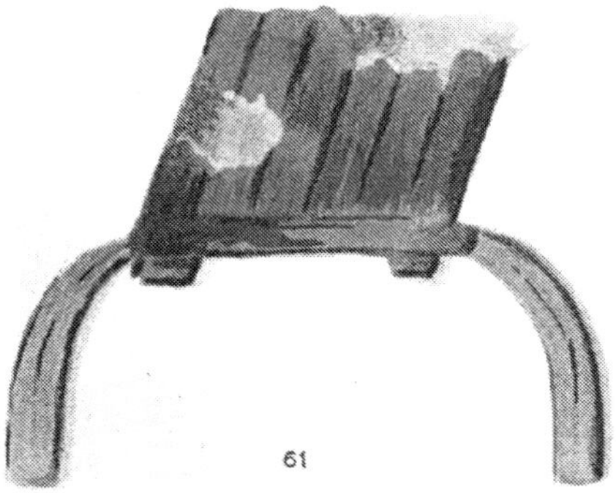

61

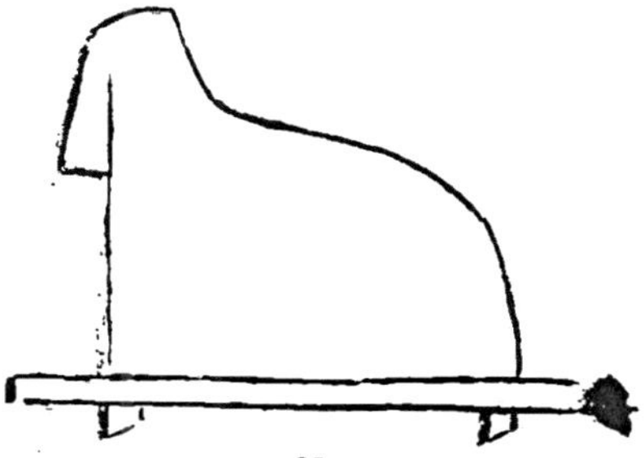

65

66

67

68

69

70

71

72

73

74

75

76

77

78

79

80

81

82

83

84

85

86

87

88

89

90

91

92

93

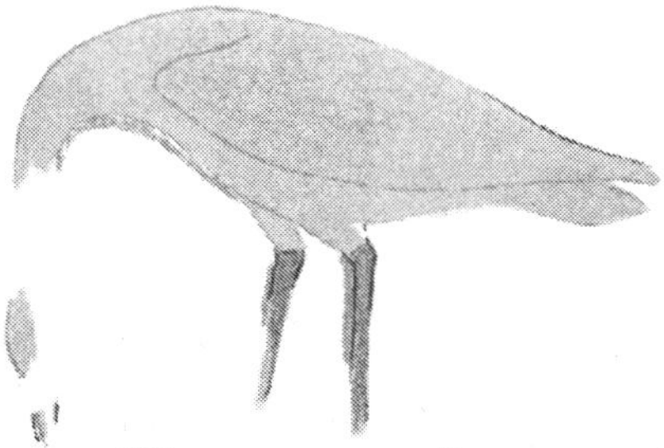

99

94

97

100

95

96

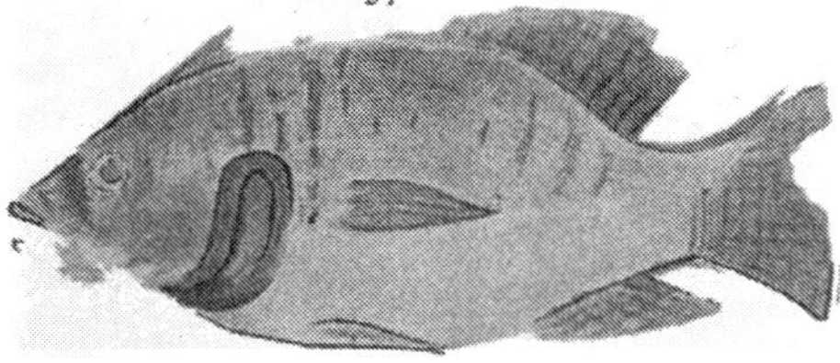
98

101

102

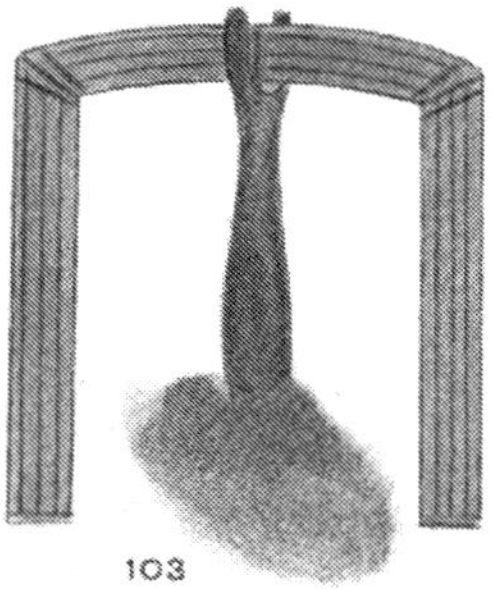
103

104

105

106

84–89, M.W.B.
90–106, H.C.

Scale ½ EL BERSHEH, TOMB OF TEHUTIHOTEP. H.C.

Scale ⅓ EL BERSHEH, TOMB OF TEHUTIHOTEP. H.C.